ON
ANY
GIVEN
DAY

JOHN F. BLAIR, PUBLISHER

Winston-Salem, North Carolina

On Any Given Day

BY

Joe Martin and Ross Yockey

Published by John F. Blair, Publisher

*The paper in this book meets the guidelines
for permanence and durability of the
Committee on Production Guidelines for
Book Longevity of the Council on
Library Resources.*

Library of Congress Cataloging-in-Publication Data
Martin, Joe, 1940–
On any given day / by Joe Martin and Ross Yockey.
p.   cm.
Includes index.
ISBN 0-89587-233-1 (alk. paper)
1. Martin, Joe, 1940–Health. 2. Amyotrophic lateral sclerosis–Patients–North
Carolina–Biography. I. Yockey, Ross. II. Title.
RC406.A24 M325 2000
616.8'3–dc21
[B]   00-044436

*Photograph used on the jacket and pages ii and iii
© Richard Charles Starling
Design by Debra Long Hampton*

For

DENNIS AND JUDY ROGERS
and our Charlotte support group

Prologue

T HE FIRST BIT OF REALITY I encounter every morning is this: I cannot move my head from the pillow or move my legs toward the edge of the bed. Yet by midmorning, I am part of a team that believes it can move the world.

That daily transformation is in part the nature of my company, NationsBank, now known as Bank of America. It is in part the triumph of a community of support that has gathered around me. And it is in large part the result of a deliberate program of recovery that is applicable to many of life's serious setbacks.

I have ALS, amyotrophic lateral sclerosis, Lou Gehrig's disease, diagnosed in October 1994. There is no cure and no significant treatment. Statistics say most people die within three to five years after diagnosis. In my case, I was told to prepare for death in less than two years.

What we have learned, my friends and I, is that it is possible to live a full, active, satisfying life despite being given a "death notice" and now despite severe paralysis. It is possible to "recover" from an incurable disease. It is possible to recover life and to remain—or become—fully engaged in life. And the techniques we have used are applicable to many of life's traumas: the death of someone close, the breakup of a marriage, the loss of a job, an unbearable disappointment, a failure in school or at work, a debilitating disease.

I am certain that life is a gift and that life is to be cherished—in the face of disappointment, in the face of disability, in the face of pain, even in the face of death.

We can do that by deliberately filling our lives with "love, hope, faith, joy, laughter, festivity, sense of purpose, determination, and will to live," as Norman Cousins proposes in *Head First: The Biology of Hope*. Those are the tools of recovery, the elements of health, the signs of faith. With them, we can strengthen and enrich our lives, no matter what the circumstances may be.

When Baltimore Orioles third baseman Cal Ripken broke Lou Gehrig's "unbreakable" record for consecutive games played, he was surprised by the national adulation it brought. "All I ever did," he said, "was get up every morning, go to the ballpark, and do my very best."

Some of us cannot get up and go to the ballpark every day. Some of us cannot even get up. But all of us can, with the help of family and friends, build personal ballparks in which to play out our lives. If we build with love, hope, faith, and the other tools suggested by Norman Cousins, we can find the power to carry on, day after day after day.

Beside my bed, I have a card that I see when I wake up. It combines the Psalms of King David with the words of Cal Ripken:

> This is the day
> The Lord has made:
> Get up.
> Go to the ballpark,
> And do your very best.

I am not as good as Cal Ripken. I do not make it every day. But at least I think about it every day. And my days are better because of the reminder—better when I get up, go to the ballpark, and find all the "love, hope, faith, joy, laughter, festivity, sense of purpose, determination, and will to live" that my family, my friends, my community, and I can create.

Joe Martin
January 2000

❧

THE FIRST TIME JOE MARTIN spoke to me, I was sitting at a round table at the rear of a large, dark hall and had no idea who he was, this small and smiling man on the stage.

He was dressed in a tuxedo and wore a tartan bow tie that gave him the appearance of a minor character in a Scott Fitzgerald novel, a sort of Scots-Presbyterian Woody Allen. He was seated in a comfortable, quaintly out-of-place desk chair at the side of the podium. In what singers call a "head voice," with very little vibration from the chest, he was speaking to more than a thousand people. He was having obvious difficulty forming his consonants, picking his way carefully through the syllables of what he had to say.

I heard him warn that fear, anger, hate, frustration, and despair were hazards to my health. Love, he said, was what I needed. Love and hope and determination. He told me tools like these could produce what he called "healing power."

The strangest word of them all, that seemed, power, from the barely functioning lips of a man so apparently powerless. What was that all about? And how could it heal?

That word heal, deep down at the tip of its Indo-European taproot, suggests the formation of wholeness. Joe, now reduced to soul, mind, eye movements, and little else, is as whole a human being as you are ever likely to meet. For Joe and for all of us, wholeness is not an achievement but a constant process. And there's Joe's power, his miracle— that he keeps on getting more whole, that he keeps on recovering, not from the disease, certainly, but from the damage it might have done to his life day by day and moment by moment.

Almost from the day he began recovering from the diagnosis of ALS, Joe aimed that power at the individuals and institutions around him. He had what the doctors call a "preexisting condition" of high visibility and community commitment, which meant that Joe's power-pebbles could cause ripples of rare and remarkable consequence. The night I first heard *him, he was not talking about his illness at all, but about how to apply the lessons of healing to the racial brokenness of the city in which we both lived.*

I understood that night, as the Urban League of Charlotte honored Joe for his achievements in the field of race relations, what Pablo Casals meant when he said, "Each man has inside him a basic decency and goodness. If he listens to it and acts on it, he is giving a great deal of what the world needs most." It took courage to do that, the ninety-year-old musician believed, and that night Joe had me agreeing. Joe Martin was listening to the goodness inside himself and acting on it, daring to be himself and daring us to do the same.

Do we dare to be ourselves? Do we dare to reject the limitations, the real and artificial "disabilities" imposed on us by birth or illness or circumstance, by education or skills or income? Do we dare to use the power within us to make whole not only ourselves but everyone we touch?

In this book, Joe writes about that power in his own life. And I have sketched in the context to reinforce the point of it all: Joe's power is the same power that you and I and anyone else can harness.

Ross Yockey
January 2000

❦

LOVE

HOPE

FAITH

JOY

LAUGHTER

FESTIVITY

SENSE OF PURPOSE

DETERMINATION

WILL TO LIVE

❦

Norman Cousins

C h a p t e r   O n e

W HEN I WOKE UP, death was tugging at
my sleeve. I could feel the pajama shirt moving just below my
elbow, like something calling me to an appointment I did not
want to keep. It was too early to be awake, but the tugging would
not let me sleep. I left Joan sleeping and went into the bathroom
to get ready to begin that awful day.

When I took off the shirt and stood in front of the mirror to
shave, I could see the muscles twitching near my elbow and in
my shoulder on the right side. I took a safety pin from a saucer
on the sink, just as three different doctors had done in their
examining rooms, and pricked myself lightly on the fingers and
along my right arm. I wasn't sure what that was supposed to
prove, to me or to the doctors, but I took some comfort from
being able to feel the sharp pinpricks, even though the twitching went on.

I was scheduled for a final report from a neurologist I had met in the course of a month of tests to determine the cause. And so I shaved and dressed and prepared to face the matter head on. By the time Joan woke up, I was having a cup of coffee and reading the newspaper, appearing to be perfectly calm.

The very first physician I had consulted about the twitching, our regular family doctor, had said I should see a neurologist. "These fasciculations can mean a number of things," he said. "We should check them out." When I was ready to leave and paying the bill, bantering happily with the nurse behind the desk, the doctor called me back into the office. "Come here," he said. "You should know that you may hear some frightening things. But there could be a lot of simple reasons for those muscles to twitch."

"What frightening things?"

"Well, somebody's going to tell you that those could be the symptoms of multiple sclerosis—MS—or of Lou Gehrig's disease." He paused and then added, "MS usually hits people at a younger age."

"I'm a lot younger than my age," I gloated, knowing that my physical fitness compulsion had impressed this doctor through the years. Still, I knew people battling MS and understood what a struggle it was. I knew nothing about Lou Gehrig's disease, though I remembered seeing a television report about a physicist who was confined to a wheelchair and unable to communicate except with the help of a computer; he had lived with the disease for twenty years or more, but his appearance was not very reassuring. Because of that television report, I knew that there was no cure for the disease. My wife and I had also heard of three people in the community who had died early and rapidly with Lou Gehrig's disease in the last several years. And somewhere in the back of my mind was a childhood memory of Lou Gehrig himself, or maybe of some actor in a movie, saying his farewell to the fans at Yankee Stadium. People were all around him, and they were all brushing back tears (so it must have been a movie and not the real Yankees, whom I had only heard on the radio).

"Let's get the tests done," my doctor had said. "Nothing to worry about, really. We just need to check it out. I'll set up some appointments." Then he added, looking at the nurse, "This week."

The tests, at the hands of a variety of doctors, had amounted to a string of false positives. Strong reflexes had turned out to be a bad sign: "Too strong," each doctor had said with the same frown, and without any explanation. Blood work and urinalysis showed no signs of lead poisoning or other abnormalities, which was also bad: "We're running out of other possibilities." A cervical MRI confirmed that my nerves were not pinched, more bad good news. "We could have fixed that," said the doctor to whom I was then sent for an EMG (electromyography).

As it turned out, Lou Gehrig's disease was diagnosed through the process of elimination. When all other possibilities were ruled out, Lou Gehrig's was the final answer.

Certain tests each doctor wanted to do again for himself, apparently unwilling to accept the mounting evidence accumulated from a succession of other doctors. Stripped to my underwear in each office, I was told to walk in a straight line with one foot immediately in front of the other, to stand straight and still with my eyes open, to hold my arms straight out, to count the fingers the doctor held up, to count backwards from a hundred, subtracting by sevens. I squeezed each doctor's fingers as hard as I could, learning each time that my left hand was very strong.

"Are you right-handed?" each one wanted to know.

And for each one, I held my arms against my chest and tried to resist the doctor's effort to pull them down. Some doctors pulled the right arm down with no apparent effort, while others strained and grimaced and were unable to move it. I thought I was learning more about the doctors than they were learning about me. Nobody budged the left arm: a victory for me and the Nautilus equipment.

"Have you always been right-handed?" each one wanted to know.

The doctor who administered the EMG, whom I had not met before and never saw again, showed the truth in his face. A young and fit-looking man with a slight speech impediment, he seemed at ease only after we were closed into the small room that housed his equipment. Disconnected television monitors and tuning boards littered the shelves and tables of the room; wires trailed off the shelves, and others crossed the room overhead to the backs of other pieces of equipment on other shelves. It looked like the garage of a teenage ham radio operator.

This doctor was unable to open my closed fist, unable to pull either of my arms down, unable to move either leg when he told me to "re-e-e . . . resist." The doctor's grimace looked contrived, but I triumphantly resisted.

The EMG had been described to me as "something they do with a needle," which turned out to be precisely correct but dramatically understated. The single needle was stuck into the

muscle tissue between my thumb and forefinger and maneu-
vered back and forth to the proper depth, the doctor saying,
"Now, re-e-e . . . relax," while the machine to which the nerve
impulses were sent set up a loud static noise, as if the doctor
might be about to invent wireless broadcasting. "Squee-e-e . . .
squeeze your thumb and finger together. Now, re-e-e . . . relax," he said as he pulled the needle out a little and then pushed
it in another millimeter. The machine went silent.

The doctor looked at the attending nurse, then hit the machine with the butt of his hand. The static started again. "I thought
they fixed it," he said to the nurse.

"They said they did," she answered.

Then the doctor pulled the needle out and stuck it quickly
into the fleshy part of my palm. "Pu-u . . . push against my
hand," he said as he pressed down on the thumb. "Now, re-e-e .
. . relax." He pushed the needle farther into the muscle. Then
the needle came out and went back in near the elbow.

"I could relax a lot better if you'd make up your mind where
you want the needle to be," I said.

The doctor didn't smile or even look up, but rather moved
the needle up to my shoulders before starting on my legs, as if
he were working on a cadaver.

"Can you tell me anything?" I asked after the needle had at
last been put away and I was sitting again on the side of the
examining table.

"Do-o-o . . . do you have an appointment for a re-e-e . . .
report?" the doctor answered.

"Yes, but not for ten days."

"That's ti-i-i . . . time enough," he said as he packed up the last of his loose pieces of equipment and started toward the door.

"Doctor," I said to keep him from leaving. "I'm scared," I then blurted out.

The young doctor paused but did not look at me, concentrating instead on the door handle in front of him. "Be-e-e . . . be sure to follow up at your reg . . . regular appointment," he said and walked out of the room, closing the door behind him.

I sat on that examining table, alone in a room that looked like the back of a garage, stifling tears, breathing quickly, and then concentrating on deep breaths. I decided that I could not go to the final report alone. I would ask Joan to come with me.

Ten days later, I sat on the edge of another examining table, waiting for the final report alone, because the nurse suggested that Joan stay for a few minutes in the waiting room. "One more examination, I guess," I said to my wife. "I'll get them to call you when that's over."

But there was no exam. The physician, whom I nicknamed "Dr. Goofy" for his incessant have-a-nice-day half-smile, sat down just beyond arm's reach. "Mr. Martin," he said, glancing up from the clipboard he clutched in front of him and smiling goofily, "you have a progressive degenerative"—I was focused on the fact that the doctor who was now pronouncing sentence, smiling at me from behind his clipboard, had never asked my first name or whether I had a wife or children, had only asked about my work and any "unusual" hobbies that might involve difficult or repetitive movements or contact with suspicious substances; it turned out that he was not actually interested in either my hobbies or my work—"disease of the central nervous system. It is sometimes called motor neuron disease, or amyotrophic lateral sclerosis. There are no treatments for this disease, but there are studies under way up at Wake Forest School of Medicine. I have a letter here," he said, holding up the letter as proof, "and I called them this morning. Their study group is full, but it will be reported in a month or two, so it doesn't matter whether you are a participant or not."

I heard almost none of what the doctor said except "progressive degenerative" and a droning slur of consonants culminating in "participant or not." I did not recognize the disease's names.

"Is that the same as Lou Gehrig's disease?" I asked.

"Yes," the doctor said, still smiling blandly, still sitting beyond reach, still clutching the clipboard with all the reassuring medical proof of his diagnosis. He sat motionless as my arms rose involuntarily over my head, hiding my face. My stifled, wrenching half-sobs were the only sound in the room.

I was surprised at my reaction. The diagnosis was not entirely unexpected, after all, and I had imagined, had actually practiced, a more restrained response. With difficulty, I returned to the script I had prepared and said, more blurted than I intended, "Could my wife come in?"

"Is she here?" asked Dr. Goofy. I could only nod and motion toward the waiting room. The doctor stood up, opened the door, and gestured for me to go and get her myself, then retreated to his office across the hall. I needed my wife desperately. I knew that her strength always shored me up when I felt weak. I also knew that I could not bear to tell her this news myself.

When Joan and I were both seated on the table in the little examining room, the doctor returned and sat again in the chair against the wall. Flashing his little smile, and without any introduction or greeting, he began to read again from his clipboard, repeating the diagnosis of a "progressive degenerative disease of the central nervous system," acknowledging the absence of any cure or any treatment, and then holding up the letter from Wake Forest School of Medicine to reinforce his claim regarding the research under way, research that he described in dry technical detail.

Joan, blond and still good looking at the age of fifty-three, sat rigidly straight, her long legs crossed at the ankle and swinging slowly from the high table. The doctor should have been stunned by this vision facing him, I thought, but he appeared not to notice who it was to whom he was giving his recitation. I noticed. And I noticed that her legs began swinging faster, although her face was frozen.

"I don't understand anything that you just said," Joan said very slowly when the doctor finished. I put my arm around her, but she did not lean toward me. The doctor studied his clipboard, apparently wondering what he had said wrong.

"I have Lou Gehrig's disease," I said to Joan, suddenly projecting the calm and self-confident character I had planned to have in this circumstance. "But the doctor seems to think it's okay," I added, recognizing at once that my demeanor was admirable but that the substance of my comment was nonsense. Still, that is what the doctor's own demeanor seemed to convey.

Joan did not look at me but continued to stare straight ahead, her legs now motionless. "How can it be okay?" she said, apparently to the doctor.

"I think it's very early in the course of the disease," he said. "And there is some research going on at Wake Forest," he added, waving the letter again, as if she would believe it only if she could see the proof. "People live a very long time with motor neuron disease."

I wondered why the doctor refused to call it by a name we might recognize. And I wondered if he could possibly be serious, since everything I had heard about this disease was, as our family doctor had promised, frightening. "A long time?" I asked tentatively. I was afraid to ask for a timetable, though I hoped that there might be some integrity in the doctor's indifferent demeanor, depending on what he actually believed about the disease.

"A long time," said Dr. Goofy, not smiling.

"Years?"

"Years."

"Long years?"

"Long years."

I decided to leave it at that. I gave Joan a little squeeze. "What should we do?" I asked the doctor.

"Nothing," he said.

"Life as normal?"

"Yes, life as normal."

"If I have a headache, just take an aspirin?"

"Yes, if you have a headache, take an aspirin."

"Can I exercise?" Yes. "Can I still work the Nautilus machines?" Yes. "Can I still run?" Yes. "Well, I'm going to run the marathon!" I squeezed Joan again. The doctor had no reaction, not knowing that my running route through the neighborhood amounted to barely a tenth of a marathon. "Do I just get up and go to the office in the morning?"

"Get up and go to the office in the morning." The doctor was answering the questions without consulting his clipboard, but he sounded like an android checking input against his data bank and feeding back the confirmations.

"Well, tonight we're going to *Grease*," I said.

"Greece?!" The android's eyes gave away his misunderstanding. "Tonight?!" he asked with something very close to animation.

"*Grease*," I said. "The musical. We have tickets for tonight. I think we'll go."

"Oh." Dr. Goofy accepted the clarification without comment.

As the doctor suggested we schedule another appointment in three months—three months!—I was recovering my confidence. I was beginning to feel okay.

Joan, on the other hand, was evidently not yet there. She had not relaxed her posture. She was still sitting rigidly on the examining table, staring at the doctor, ignoring my gentle squeezes. As the doctor exited the room, her eyes followed him. And she gave him the finger.

I nearly fell off the examining table. My beautiful wife, that gentle and caring and loving creature, she who had never said an unkind word about anybody in the whole world, the very model for Miss Congeniality, had just reacted to a medical diagnosis by flipping the bird at the neurologist who delivered it.

"Now I feel better," she said. She slipped off the table and offered me her hand to help me down.

༺࿐༻

Joe and Joan met in 1963 at the University of Minnesota. Joan, a recently graduated cheerleader and homecoming queen, was dating the college football hero and working as a bank teller, training to become a manager. Joe, abandoning a very brief career selling insurance in favor of pursuing a master's degree in American studies, had found his way from South Carolina to Minnesota. To support himself, he took a job as "house mother" at Delta Tau Delta fraternity.

One evening, so the story goes, Nancy Jo Kohan, fiancée of the Delt president, was surprised to find Joe without a date. When Joe expressed a lack of enthusiasm for any of the sorority girls he'd met, she asked him to describe the sort of woman he was looking for. To Joe's regret, Nancy Jo knew no one meeting his description of the perfect woman.

Until, that is, the next day at lunchtime, when Nancy Jo rushed to the fraternity house. She couldn't wait to give Joe her news. Just that morning, she had been working at the registration desk for new education students, and who should walk up but Joan Werness. They had not seen each other since Girls' State five years earlier. Now, Joan was going to give up banking and become a teacher. And by the way, Nancy Jo told Joe, "she is the girl you described last night. Here's her phone number."

That night, Joe made a telephone call, introduced himself, and asked her if she'd meet him on campus.

Joan, intrigued by his low and lilting, almost foreign-sounding Southern accent, accepted. "How will I know you?" she asked. "Will you have a rose behind your ear?"

Joe replied, "Or between my teeth."

Joan was standing in a crowd on the steps of the education building when she saw Joe approaching across the lawn with a long-stemmed rose in his grin, raising his eyebrows hopefully at every attractive girl he passed. Mortified, she ducked behind a column to plan her escape. Joe vanished into the building, where he handed Nancy Jo Kohan the rose and gave a shrug. Quickly, she led him back outside and delivered him up to Joan. Nancy Jo kept the flower while Joe and Joan went off for ice cream. They got to know each other over cones of butter brickle on the main quad.

By Christmastime, Joe knew Nancy Jo Kohan had been right. Joan Werness really was the girl he had described. He had met the girl he wanted to marry. Trouble was, all the sparks seemed to be flying in one direction. At home for the holidays, Joe sought the advice of his brother Jim and sister-in-law Dottie. The three sat down at the breakfast-room table and talked strategy. Not taking any chances, Jim wrote out a script for Joe to follow.

Back in Minneapolis, Joe tracked down Joan and asked how soon she could go out with him. She demurred, as the scriptwriter had predicted she would. She was going to be "tied up" for the next several weekends. There were other guys ahead of Joe. Following the script, Joe firmly declared that if he had to wait that long to see her again, he'd better just go ahead and break things off.

Joan had never read the script but nevertheless adhered perfectly to the writer's analysis of her character. She could not bring herself to make someone unhappy. "Well, I'm not busy Thursday," she said.

Thursday evenings were soon supplemented with Sunday dinners at *her parents' home. In six weeks, they were engaged to be married. The date was set: August 15, 1964, less than a year after Nancy Jo Kohan had identified Joe's perfect girl.*

Thirty years later, holding hands, they left the doctor's office with a diagnosis of Lou Gehrig's disease and a plan to spend the evening together at a stage production of Grease.

Chapter Two

G*REASE WAS NOISY*. And fun. We laughed, we clapped, we sang along. And when we were home, we kissed. We had met the challenge of Day One, and we were ready to face the morning.

But in the morning, the twitching seemed worse. I stared at it in the bathroom mirror, then sat in a chair beside the bed and put my legs up on the mattress and stared at them. For half an hour, I stayed perfectly still, staring at my legs. Nothing. All the twitching was in my right arm. There, it was constant, sometimes pulsing, sometimes rolling, as if some alien life form had taken up residence and wanted out. It never completely stopped. Once or twice, out of the corner of my eye, I thought I might have seen a twitch in my left shoulder, but I never caught it in full view. Dr. Goofy had not said much about the twitching, only that cutting back on caffeine would reduce it.

If dropping caffeine was his way of reducing stimulation of my nerves, his expectations were about to be blown away. My nerves and I were about to meet our own Dr. Doom.

My brother Jim, a former governor of North Carolina and also a former chemistry professor with a Ph.D. from Princeton, had taken a job as vice president for research at Carolinas Medical Center. He responded to my diagnosis with predictably partisan confidence in his medical center, as opposed to the one with which my diagnosing doctor was affiliated. But he also responded as a brother—an older brother accustomed to taking care of things—and a governor accustomed to calling in favors in an emergency. He set up an appointment with a neurologist at his medical center. I figured a second opinion wouldn't hurt.

And so I went through the standard drill again. I paraded in front of my brother and the doctor, walking in a straight line with one foot immediately in front of the other; I stood straight and still with my eyes open, holding my arms straight out; I counted the fingers the doctor held up and counted backwards from a hundred, subtracting by sevens. I was more conscious of being evaluated by Jim than by yet another neurologist—especially as an English major trying to do subtraction. I concentrated, but the doctor was not listening to the arithmetic.

"Is that your natural voice?" he wanted to know. I'm a fairly deep bass. I was a double bass at a younger age in my college chorus. People often commented about my voice, but nobody had ever asked if it was "natural." I wondered what this doctor thought that might mean, but I just nodded yes. "Is it always that low?" he challenged. I looked at Jim, a tenor, then smiled and nodded again. "It seems a little hoarse," the doctor said.

The doctor told me to stick out my tongue. "Can you hold it still?" he asked. I was already holding it still, but I pointed it more obviously. "Try to relax it." I could do one or the other but not both.

Despite my impatience at jumping through all these familiar hoops again, I liked this man immediately. We had never met, but we had many mutual friends. He was well known and well liked. He was, in fact, a wonderful man, warm and personable. He smiled reassuringly, he patted me on the shoulder, he touched my knee, and he told me I was going to die.

The diagnosis confirmed, the doctor pronounced the sentence. "You are going to read that people with ALS generally live three to five years. Don't believe it," he said. "Two years," he announced with certainty. And then he added, "In your case, twenty months."

Pleasantly but insistently, this kindly physician took me straight to the end game. Without my asking, he explained the predictable course of paralysis and described how I would die. The bottom line: comfortably. And soon.

By the time Jim and I walked to our cars, my bravado was gone. Jim said nothing. Instead of telling me good-bye, he climbed into the passenger seat of my Explorer. I looked at him, and I cried.

Joan and I decided not to tell anyone about the diagnosis until we could tell our children face to face. We didn't want to run the risk of having them hear accidentally from someone other than us. We would have to wait until Thanksgiving, which was almost five weeks away.

The result was that we were alone with the information and had no way to deal with it. Worse, we were alone separately when it mattered most.

Throughout our thirty years together, any weakness in either of us had triggered a compensating strength in the other. We were very good at picking each other up. Under the stress of my diagnosis, neither of us wanted to face the world alone. Anytime we left the house, we were practically joined at the shoulder.

At home, though, especially after the twenty-month prognosis, we were afraid to talk to or even look at each other. I would find Joan playing solitaire on the computer—for hours. And when she was busy with something else, I played solitaire. Neither of us interrupted the other. It was the most miserable time of our lives.

For the first time, I knew real fear—gripping, unremitting fear. I did not want to show it, did not want to admit it—and could not get rid of it.

I had read that ALS could take away my voice, and I recognized that the hoarseness I had denied in the doctor's office was now getting worse. That hoarseness and the twitching in my tongue had undoubtedly led him to his dire prediction. The effect on me went far beyond the issue of life expectancy. My voice was a major part of my identity, and communication was not only my career but my approach to life. I thought I could bear any burden imaginable if only I could talk about it. And I thought that no matter what might happen to my body, I would still be me as long as I sounded like me. So the increasing hoarseness terrified me.

One night, watching television alone while Joan was upstairs, I started repeating what was being said on screen and listening to my voice. I could not prevent the tears. I walked into the darkened back room and, looking out into woods I could not see, I rasped, "Please, God, no!" It was possibly the most authentic prayer I had ever uttered.

Sleep had never been difficult for me. It was what I did best under stress. But the good doctor had explained that I would die in my sleep—peacefully, he said, in the early-morning hours, when my metabolism was at its lowest. So now, I was afraid to go to sleep. I would delay going to bed until Joan was asleep and I could not keep my eyes open. And after a few hours of sleep, I would wake up, worry about my metabolism, and stay awake until dawn.

I did not—and do not—think I was afraid of death as a personal thing. But I was worried about managing the process gracefully, and I could not bear the sadness it would cause. Lying awake in the dark of those early-morning hours, I would imagine Joan and the children at my funeral, and I would cry, trying hard not to shake the bed. I felt guilty over what I was about to do to my family.

Despite my attempted restraint, I was so shaken one afternoon when I was upstairs alone in the bedroom staring at my fasciculations—those incessant twitches—that I could not stop crying. I went downstairs with tears streaming down my face, found Joan in the kitchen, pulled her to me as tightly as I could—because I needed her strength and because I did not want her to look at my face—and blurted out, "I'm so sorry!" It was one of the few times we had cried together; neither of us was strong enough to fake strength.

That night, Joan and I played dominoes. Together.

Over the next few days, I kept very busy getting everything "ready." I did not feel panic particularly, but I did feel urgency. And I found terrific satisfaction in getting things done. I pruned the shrubbery perfectly, so that Joan would be able to show someone how it should be done. I fixed squeaky doors. Cabinet drawers that had been sliding off their gliders for ten years suddenly became intolerable. They all got brand-new hardware.

Before the diagnosis, we had already begun the slow and tedious process of redrawing our wills. The lawyer helping us was knowledgeable and thorough. But she had very effectively convinced us that we would be in bad shape if either of us should "decease" while the old will was still in effect. So I began calling her on a daily basis to harass her about completing the process. She knew someone whose aunt had died of ALS. She said she would hurry.

On the phone with the lawyer, I thought my voice sounded firm and forceful. I went into the bathroom attached to my office and looked into the mirror. I stuck out my tongue. No twitching.

Was I being cured? Not even at the time did I think so. Was something else miraculous going on? I thought so then, and I still think so.

Sometime between my prayer in the darkened back room and my apology to Joan in the bright kitchen, maybe while I was repairing a drawer or pruning the hedge, the stress began slipping out of my life—not vanishing by any means, but subsiding. And my throat and tongue and vocal cords were relaxing, returning to normal.

The twitching in my arms did not go away. Still, I began to feel better about the prospect of getting through the night. How many nights I might make it remained an uncertainty. No matter how "gradual" the progress of the disease might be, twenty months (608 nights, by my calculation) was not a long time. And the margin of error, for all I knew, could be just as great on the short side as on the long.

My father had made a habit of kneeling beside his bed for prayer every night before going to sleep. My mother had made a habit of waiting patiently for him under the covers. It was predictable which example would carry the day with their children. I had not knelt for prayer—or even remembered to pray very often before bed—since my father stopped tucking me in.

But in November 1994, I took to kneeling on the soft carpet beside my bed. Joan waited patiently for me under the covers. Among other things, I discovered that he who kneels to pray gains the advantage of climbing into a bed that has already been warmed by the non-kneeler. I wondered if my father had counted that among his blessings.

A less happy discovery was that I did not know what to say in my prayer. I am certain that my father's prayers were not memorized or even formulaic, but beautiful extemporaneous anthems of devotion about whatever was on his heart. But when I tried to express my own feelings, I found no words.

The first night, I managed to say exactly nothing. Joan did not ask me what I was doing. She just hugged me when I got into bed.

The next night, something came to me, and I began,

Now I lay me down to sleep;
I pray thee, Lord, my soul to keep.

It did not seem funny at all. I could hear my father's voice saying the words, could practically feel his hand on my shoulder. Then I hit the line that took me apart:

If I should die before I wake . . .

As a child, I had hated that line. I always left it out if no one was listening. Now, facing the prospect of fewer than 608 nights and the doctor's assurance that on one of those nights I would, in fact, die before I woke, the reality of my situation was unavoidable. Leaving out the line was no longer an option. But crying kept me from going on with the prayer. It took several nights to get past that line. When I completed it, I was certain that I meant it.

If I should die before I wake,
I pray thee, Lord, my soul to take.

If I should live another day . . .

Trouble again. I knew what was coming:

I pray thee, Lord, to guide my way.

And I knew in the split second before it came that I was not prepared to say it. I knew that I was not, in fact, living my life as if I expected God to "guide my way." It took me several more nights to get through that barrier. If I wanted to be serious about "my soul to take," I had to be equally serious about "guide my way."

As I had instinctively known from the beginning of this journey, "If I should die before I wake" would not be the greatest challenge to me. What if I made it through the night? "If I should live another day," would I have the skill, the grace, the boldness, the humility to let God "guide my way"? Would I even know what that meant?

When at last I was able to say the whole prayer, I found it not quite satisfying. Something important was missing. So I crafted another couplet, in language that I presumed to be consistent with the era of the original prayer:

> *Whate'er betide this life of mine,*
> *My friends and family, Lord, be thine.*

Sleep—deep, solid, unworried sleep—is wonderful. And waking up fully rested is even better.

It is hard to beat waking up in the morning as an antidote to death. Doing it for several mornings in a row brings an expectation that it might just keep happening—if not indefinitely, at least again. I began to think I could see through the night into tomorrow, maybe even as far as the day after tomorrow.

Mornings became a thrill for me. I began sleeping until first light, then getting up, dressing in gym shorts, stretching, and hitting the sidewalk for a run through the neighborhood. I loved the exhilaration of that morning run.

Over dominoes in the evenings, Joan and I made plans to tell the children. Elizabeth, home from a year in Ecuador after graduating from Duke, had now left again for a year in Washington State in search of more mountains. She could not be enticed home without knowing the truth, and she would need to be able to talk with her brothers immediately, so she would have to be told afterward and by telephone. David would be home from his freshman year at Denison University early in Thanksgiving week. No matter what we planned, he would spend most of his time finding his high-school buddies; it was critical that they not know anything that might accidentally slip out to David prematurely. Older brother Joe B., a Davidson graduate and now a senior at Union Theological Seminary in Virginia, would be home on Wednesday of that week. He would bring his wife, Jodi, whose father had been diagnosed with multiple sclerosis at the age of twenty-four and had survived in a happy and functional family for thirty years, though he was now severely paralyzed. We would wait for Joe B. and Jodi. That would put us at our house at Lake Norman, the best possible place for such news.

The lake is where we have shared summers for years with the families of Jim and Dottie Martin and our close friends Tony and Susan Abbott. In fact, we are so close that the Abbott and Martin children think they are all cousins. We live in a little compound of sorts and share everything from a swimming dock and a ski boat to rental movies and iced tea. For meals and special occasions, we are almost always together. Thanksgiving would be such a time, cozy and familiar and supportive.

In the meantime, we each needed someone to tell. Our only unguarded social life was occasional evenings with Jim and Dottie, who had been my friend since we were in high school together. With them, we could relax, not minding if they saw the muscles twitch in my arm, not minding if they saw emotions spill over. They were a safe harbor for us.

But neither of us could hide the truth any longer from the people closest to us every day. Joan would tell Marilyn Svenson, her childhood-through-college friend who had moved to Charlotte, and Jean Finkelstein, her comrade in arms through many years of teaching preschool. I would tell Chuck Cooley, personnel executive at the company now known as Bank of America, who had the office next to mine on the fifty-seventh floor and who had been my friend and coach since I came to the bank twenty years earlier. I would also tell my boss, Hugh McColl, chairman and CEO of the company. I had already told Nancy Dry, administrative assistant for both Chuck and me and my office friend for all those twenty years, because I needed her support just to get through each day at the office.

To call Hugh my boss is to miss the point of his relationship with me or with any other person. He has the same role at the office that he has in the neighborhood or anywhere else: he assumes that he's in charge. He is also totally dependent on all of us for whom he is responsible, and he is fiercely devoted to the relationships that make all this symbiosis possible.

Hugh McColl did not flinch at my news. Flinching is not part of his program anyway, but I suspected that Chuck had forewarned him. He asked me what I knew about ALS and pronounced my response "unimpressive."

"We've got to know more," he said, reaching for the phone. He asked his associate Pat Hinson to get the city's senior neurologist on the line, then waited for it to happen. "They've got telephones on the goddamn golf course," he said into the phone in reaction to whatever he had heard. "Tell them I want to talk to him right now." The good doctor was on the phone in minutes.

When Hugh hung up, he reported that the doctor did not know much about ALS and did not think there was anyone else in Charlotte who had much experience with it. "He'll find out who's the best in the country and let us know."

No transaction with Hugh is noncompetitive. I took the challenge. The doctor who had given me the bad prognosis had also argued in favor of action; Dr. Doom was now transformed into Dr. Do-Something. He expressed a genuine concern for his patient and an action-oriented attitude unknown among the neurologists who diagnose most cases of ALS. He recognized a name on a list of specialists—his former teacher at Duke, who now ran an ALS clinic in Houston sponsored by the Muscular Dystrophy Association. He called to report that he was able to get an appointment almost immediately; we would leave for Houston on the Sunday after Thanksgiving.

When Hugh came by a couple of days later, he had the name of "the best ALS doctor in the world: Stanley Appel." I turned over the card for my Houston appointment and handed it to him. "Stanley Appel," it said. Hugh is good, but I had beaten him.

When Joan met with Dottie Martin and Susan Abbott to plan Thanksgiving dinner, she could not hide her feelings from

Susan. Susan canceled her plans for the remainder of the day and came with Joan to meet me for lunch at our house.

Susan was shocked, she was sympathetic, she was sad. She was not daunted. "Have you read Bob Stone's book?" she wanted to know. I had not.

Stone was a classmate of mine at Davidson College and later a neighbor of Susan and Tony's. Diagnosed with pancreatic cancer and given only a short time to live, he had decided to fight. He recruited friends to help. They adopted the buffalo—a tough animal, part of a dying breed that is making a comeback—as their mascot. His book about his remarkable experience was called *Where the Buffalos Roam: Gathering Teams to Face Life's Crises.* Susan and Tony had been early and ardent buffalos, creating joy and laughter and confidence in Bob and Genie Stone's life.

About the same time Bob was diagnosed with cancer, another Davidson friend developed a brain tumor. Buddy Kemp had been my pledge brother in our fraternity and had become president of our company. He was the most admirable person I knew, both as a friend and as a business associate. Buddy had survived heart disease at approximately the same age at which his father had died of a heart attack. He was resilient, aggressive, successful. But when he told me about the tumor in his brain, he was resolved that he would not live long—longer than the doctors thought, but not long.

As the communications officer for his company and also as his friend, I became his staff assistant for dealing with communications about his condition. I handled news releases and media inquiries, wrote up his idea for a scholarship program he wanted to establish at Davidson, drew up plans for his funeral, and wrote his obituary—all of which documents he wanted to see and approve in advance, the same way he ran his part of the company.

"This is the first time I have ever edited an obituary," he said when he returned the draft to me.

"Well, it's the first time I've written one for someone who still has opinions," I told him.

Buddy took all of us through his experience of death. He never denied what was happening to him, and he did not shield his friends from the truth. I was overwhelmed by his courage, his integrity, his compassion, and, more than all else, his grace. And I resented the contrasting example of Bob Stone's audacious fight. I was never quite a full member of the buffalo herd.

But when I finally read Stone's book at Susan's insistence, I found not bluster but common sense. It seemed to me that his approach was psychologically sound and theologically solid. In a very different way, he exhibited courage, integrity, compassion, and, yes, grace.

"Will you talk to Bob?" Susan asked several days later.

"Well, okay," I said, worried about how I would control my emotions while breaking my news to him.

"Good," she said. "I told him about your diagnosis this afternoon. He'll call you after supper."

And so I took the call, the same one received by hundreds of other people, both friends and strangers, whom Bob called in the pit of their fear and despair. He was all business in the beginning. "Hell of a thing, ain't it?" "Who's your doctor?" "What do you know about who's doing research on ALS?" "Well, first thing we have to do is find the best place in the world for treating what you've got. You can leave that to me."

When the program of action was settled, Bob became a cheer-leader. "You and I really lucked out on wives, didn't we?" His voice was strong, his laugh hearty and infectious. "Isn't it terrific that you and I had parents who prepared us for this kind of thing?" "I hear your children are doing great." "Listen, I've got some stuff I want you to see. One's a video of an interview CBS News did with Genie and me. And one's a book that Norman Cousins wrote. I'll send it to you. I'm not sending you my book. You can go out and buy that one." The big laugh again.

Bob Stone had been a crackerjack life-insurance salesman. On the phone with me that night, he was just selling life.

Susan came up with a copy of the Norman Cousins book, so I started reading it immediately. *Head First: The Biology of Hope*, it was called. From the dust jacket, I learned that Cousins had also written *Anatomy of an Illness*, a book in which he claimed to have raised all the right questions. "This new one," he wrote, "has all the right answers."

The premise of *Head First* was simple. We have known for a long time that anger, fear, anxiety, despair, and frustration are bad for our health. Why is it so hard to believe that love, hope, faith, joy, laughter, festivity, sense of purpose, determination, and will to live are good for us?

Jim and Dottie, Susan, Tony, Hugh, Chuck, Nancy, Marilyn, Jean: we had the beginnings of a powerhouse team. On Monday morning of Thanksgiving week, while I was out running, I de-cided it was time to start building. I mentally composed a letter to our friends, letting them know what we were dealing with and asking their help. My only misgivings had to do with telling Joan the plan and running into her Norse suck-it-up reserve.

At home, while I was recording my split times in my running journal, Joan said, "Susan called while you were out. She thinks you should write a letter to tell people what's going on."

Writing the letter had an unexpected benefit. It forced us to put our feelings into words, and those words became the basis of our conversation with the children the day before Thanksgiving. That conversation—planned for the morning, when we would be rested and have plenty of daylight ahead of us—was more emotional than we had hoped, and we were glad to have the letter in our heads to guide us through it.

As I spluttered through the explanation, David stepped up and hugged me. "We love you, Dad," he said. I could not answer.

As Joan and Jodi joined in, Joe B. hugged us all and said, "And we know you love us, too, Dad."

After talking to Elizabeth on the phone, Joan and I left the children all on the line to speak to each other without us. Then the boys and I played Frisbee golf—just because we could.

That afternoon, we dropped the letters in the mail.

November 25, 1994

Dear Friends:

For the past several weeks, Joan and I have been struggling with a tough situation relating to my health. We hate to burden you with the news, but we believe that your knowing about it will be a great help to us.

I have been diagnosed with ALS (amyotrophic lateral sclerosis, better known as "Lou Gehrig's disease"). ALS is a neuromuscular disease of unknown cause that leads to progressive muscular paralysis over time. There is no cure or treatment, although there is a great deal of research under way.

The condition proceeds at an unpredictable pace in different people. There are notable examples of people living productively with it for fifteen or twenty years, but the reality of the disease is that it generally runs its course over a much shorter period of time. There is no pain associated with the condition, and no mental disability. It is not contagious in any way.

Joan and I are finding that we have much to be thankful for—especially that we are very good at helping each other "up" from the "down" times this news still brings to us now and then. We have a very positive attitude toward coping with the situation, and we want you to know two things in particular:

1. My life has been blessed way beyond the matter of how many years I have. (Many of those blessings are on the address list for this letter!) Even with this condition that I now have, my life is very, very good. I haven't lost sight of that for a moment, and it has helped me already to deal with the diagnosis and to be able to enjoy the good days that we continue to have.

2. We need you. We need your prayers, your love, your caring. Our love for you and our certainty of your love for us are what causes us to reach out to you with this news. We believe very strongly that God's sustaining care will be brought to us through the fellowship of family and friends—in whose love we can see and know God's love. A good hug is great theology!

You should know something else very important: I feel good. I work out or run every day. It is one way I can get myself in shape to deal with this condition when it begins to develop, and it makes me feel terrific in the meantime.

So I'm pursuing my fitness program religiously (literally—I work out at the new gym at our church). I expect to continue in my job at the bank (among my blessings: a wonderful place to work and a group of wonderful people who work with me; they may find my attention erratic now and then, but they would probably say that there's nothing new about that). I am also due to be clerk of session at our church for 1995, and I have no reason to think I cannot do that; I am looking forward to it especially since an old friend, John Rogers, arrives in January to be our new minister. And I will keep writing when I have time. (My first *published* short story will appear in the next issue of the *Crescent Review*—I can't resist mentioning it; I'm really excited about it.) I do not know what a positive attitude can do about ALS, but it sure makes each day a lot better.

When you get this letter, Joan and I will be in Houston at the Texas Medical Center for a week of intensive evaluation and diagnosis. Among other things, we will learn more about how to deal with this disease, and we will learn whether there are research projects or experimental tests relative to my particular set of conditions that are open to my participation.

We are sorry that we could not share this news with everybody in a more personal way, but please know that you are very much in our thoughts. When we get back from Houston, we will be in touch—to cry together if we feel like it, but then to get back to the joy of just being together. We need that.

With love,

Joe

⚬✕⚬

Charlotte became home for Joe and Joan and their children, Joe B., and Elizabeth, in 1973. David was born a year later.

Joe had taken a job with a small bank that had a grandiose view of its future. He hardly fit the "banker" stereotype. His graduate degree was not an MBA but a Ph.D. in medieval English literature. Rather than a nose for the bottom line, Joe had a penchant for community activism fired in the intense political furnace of Duke University in the 1960s. Perhaps the only person who believed he might fit in with a company of bankers was Chuck Cooley, the young personnel officer who recruited Joe after serving alongside him as a volunteer in Jim Martin's first campaign for Congress.

Joe's assignment was to be the company's "corporate social responsibility officer." Exactly what that might entail, no one was quite sure in 1973. A quarter-century later, he'd hear himself called "the conscience of the company," the executive vice president "in charge of doing the right thing." But Joe would always insist that he joined the bank not because it needed a conscience but because it had one.

North Carolina National Bank grew, sometimes by leaps and bounds, sometimes by fits and stumbles, just the way Joe's job grew. Twice, he left the company, uncomfortable with his shifting role—public relations, government lobbying, internal and external communications, news management. But each time he left, he found himself missing the pace and the power, the energy of growth, the intellectual intensity of the team, the chance to make a difference in his adopted community, and he went back.

By the 1980s, he was working directly for the chairman, Tom Storrs. Equipped with his own Ph.D. (from Harvard), Storrs trained Joe to be an integral part of the company's strategic planning team. In fact, Storrs was training his whole team for larger roles that none of them then could identify. They surprised the banking world in 1982 by crossing state lines and buying banks in Florida, despite the general consensus that interstate banking was prohibited by federal law. Five years later, under the command of a new CEO, Hugh McColl, they staged an even bigger coup by taking over the largest bank in Texas. In 1992, they bought Atlanta's top bank and created NationsBank. Joe got credit for choosing the new name and engineering the change.

As the bank expanded, so did corporate social responsibility. From $300,000 a year, the company's annual charitable contributions budget increased to more than $30 million. Its community development corporation, the first one in America approved for a bank, was restoring inner-city neighborhoods. This meant enriching the residents of those neighborhoods, not removing them. With the announcement of the Atlanta merger, the company's community investment group committed the staggering sum of $10 billion for loans to people and neighborhoods that had been underserved—or underhandedly discriminated against—by the banking industry.

The team of bankers who had grown up under Storrs and McColl was now running the third-largest banking company in the country. Chuck Cooley had become principal corporate personnel officer. Joe Martin's title was principal corporate affairs officer.

Like the company of which he'd become an integral part, Joe looked to be in his prime, ready to reap the rewards of hard work and careful planning. But Joe's lower motor neurons were blowing out like overtaxed fuses, and the nerve fibers weren't getting the brain's signals to their destinations. Some of his muscles were starving. He was experiencing the early signs of what the local experts said could only be amyotrophic lateral sclerosis, Lou Gehrig's disease. In 1994, Joe's best shot at an authoritative opinion was in one of the comprehensive ALS clinics sponsored by the Muscular Dystrophy Association or the ALS Association. The closest ones to Charlotte were in Philadelphia, Cleveland, and Houston, about a thousand miles away.

Chapter   Three

N ONE OF THE DOCTORS I SAW volun-
teered any information about the actual disease they said I had.
When I mentioned this to one of them, he said there was a
brochure in his files that he could go and get if I wanted to
read it. I was not sure what they were hiding from me, but
their reluctance to talk made me reluctant to ask. I declined
the brochure.

I did ask about a support group. I thought there might be
people who could help by sharing their experience and their
method of coping. Also, I had never even seen anybody with
ALS, and I wanted to know what people with ALS looked like.

"Don't go to a support group," the doctor said. "It will just
depress you."

"Why?"

"Because this is very early in the course of your disease. You are better off than 98 percent of the people who have it."

Apparently, whatever "worse off" might entail, I was better off not looking at it, better off not knowing where I was headed. It might depress me.

I was already depressed. I felt isolated by my diagnosis, alone and vulnerable to my fears. I was falling, teetering back and forth as emotions moved me one way and then another. There was no one to hold on to except Joan. And I held on to her for dear life. Had she moved a physical or psychological inch away from me, I would have keeled over. She was steady.

At the office, Nancy protected me. She knew when I was up for a call or a visitor and when I was not. "Just like hot flashes," she said. "In the middle of one, you really don't want to have to be nice to somebody." She made my office a safe haven I could count on.

Jim, characteristically, took off like a rocket scientist. Exploring the Internet, he found more information than I could handle. The research reports fascinated him, and he related them to me, the English major, in tedious detail. They all concluded not with a bang but a whimper, providing no clues about the disease or its treatment. I asked him to start sifting the material for me, rather than funneling it all into my head. "I want only the good stuff," I told him.

It was a mystery to Jim the scientist that information could be good or bad based on its effect rather than its inherent validity, but he agreed to do as I asked. And when he got the hang of it, he was perfect. I had the feeling that *we* were leaving no stone unturned, while *I* was being kept at a safe distance from any snakes that might be unearthed.

Among the things that Jim dug up was the telephone number of the ALS Association's national headquarters in California. I did not call right away. I did not want any negative surprises. I did not even know how to start the conversation. "Hello, my name is Joe, and I have ALS"? What should I ask for? Why was I calling? All I actually wanted was to make contact. I wanted to touch ALS.

One afternoon, I secreted myself in the bedroom so no one could see me or hear me and dialed the number in California. I wanted to know how they would answer the phone, but I expected to hang up before saying anything.

"ALS Association. Can I help you?" The voice was friendly and cheerful. A young woman, I guessed. "Hello?" she said. "Can I help you?"

"My name is Joe," I said, "and I have ALS."

"Well," said the cheerful voice, "you have come to the right place."

All I could say was, "Oh, good."

"We have people who can help," she said. "And we have lots of information. Let me get a patient counselor on the line."

The counselor and I repeated the introductory dance steps.

"What can I do to help?" she said.

"I guess I really just wanted to know you're there," I said.

She laughed. "We're here. You can call anytime." She asked me when I was diagnosed, what symptoms I had, what problems I was having.

"My only problem," I said, "is that I have ALS."

She laughed again, then led me through a litany of lightweight disabilities. I had none. "We have manuals and materials for any disabilities you might encounter," she said, "but for now, let's just put you on the mailing list for our newsletter." She asked about my medical care, and I told her about my upcoming appointment with Dr. Appel in Houston. "One of the best," she said. "You're going to be in good hands." She offered to talk with me again after the trip to the clinic. "Stay in touch," she said.

I made one other call. The doctor who had told me how little time I had remaining thought I should see a physiatrist right away. I didn't even know what a physiatrist was. "It's a physical therapist with a Ph.D.," he said. He gave me the name of one who was on the approved list for my insurance plan.

In the week before going to Houston, and in another wave of depression, I called the physiatrist. He was all business—and very busy.

"My name is Joe Martin, and I have ALS," I said. I was getting better at saying it.

"What's your problem?"

"I have ALS," I said more forcefully.

"I gathered that, but what problem are you having?"

"Well, I'm having a problem with being diagnosed with ALS." I was being pulled deeper into frustration and depression by the irritated voice on the other end of the line.

"What is it that you cannot do?"

"Right now, nothing."

"Then what do you need me for?" he said.

"I was told I should have a physiatrist, and I thought I should make contact before going to a clinic next week in Houston."

"Stan Appel?" he asked.

"Yes, I guess it's his clinic."

"Do you like Chinese?"

"What?!"

"Do you eat Chinese food?" he said. I had called him for help with disabilities related to my impending death, and he wanted to talk about egg rolls. "There's a great little restaurant near Appel's office. They're famous for their dumplings."

Turns out the guy had graduated from Baylor College of Medicine and knew all about Appel, who chaired the Neurology Department there. He also knew every restaurant in Houston. "What about barbecue?" he said. Without waiting for an answer, he added, "People in North Carolina don't even know what barbecue is all about. You gotta go to Goode Company—that's pronounced like *good* but spelled G-double-o-d-with-an-e-on-the-end. Goode Company Barbecue on Kirby. Nothing like it anywhere. Now, for Italian—are you taking notes?" I was, and I was smiling. "I mean, if you have to go to Houston, you might as well have a good time. Man, I miss that place." At the end of his list of recommended restaurants, he added as an afterthought, "Oh, if you have any problems with ALS, give me a call."

Without knowing it, I presume, the hungry and homesick physiatrist had picked me up and set me back on the horse. I could hardly wait to gallop into Houston.

The Texas Medical Center is the biggest in the world. It is a separate city on the edge of the Rice University campus, a collection of hospitals, medical schools, nursing schools, institutes of various sorts, and research labs. It has more than forty thousand employees. It also has its own hotels and restaurants and banks and shops.

On Monday morning, we registered at the hospital and were shown to a private room that would be our daytime home. Because of the way insurance companies and hospitals handle charges for overnight stays, it was much cheaper to sleep at a hotel and go to the hospital as a day patient. That arrangement also left us free in the evenings to pursue our other priority in Houston: eating.

The next three days were a blur of bustling to test sites around Methodist Hospital and the Neurology Department of the Baylor College of Medicine. The lead-off lecture was delivered by Dr. Stanley Appel. He came into our room followed by a phalanx of medical students who hung on his every word. He wanted to go over a sort of orientation to what we'd be doing.

"We have been working with ALS patients for a long time," he said. "We won't know for a few days whether this is what you have, but we will need your help. This is a team approach, and you are part of the team." Stan Appel is a small but powerful-looking man, maybe sixty years old, with burning dark eyes and close-cropped black hair. His face, like his general demeanor, is serious and severe. In contrast to this intimidating austerity are the trademarks by which he is known: cowboy boots, bow tie, and woolly worms for eyebrows. "Before we start the day, do you have questions?" He smiled at my clipboard.

"How much time do you have?" I asked.

"Fire away."

As I went down my list—well, Jim's list first ("Should we

get involved with clinical trials in [a] nerve growth factors, [b] neurontin, [c] super oxide dismutase, [d] branched chain amino acids?")—he never flinched. If he suspected the truth, that I didn't know beans about dismutase or any of the other things on the list, he showed no sign of it.

He explained the theory behind each experimental trial, then concluded, "We will do what you want to do. But I will not ask you to participate in a trial that puts you at risk of being on a placebo and prevents you from using other therapies that might be helpful to you."

I knew just enough to recognize a revolutionary idea: The patient was more important than the science.

"Next?" he said, nodding at my clipboard.

Straight to my question: "What are Duke's chances against Carolina next week?"

"Nil," he said. No smile. "He's from North Carolina," he said to the students around him, then said to me about his students, "They've never heard of the schools you mentioned." A few of the students smiled. Most looked terrified. "And as for Duke's chances of beating Dean Smith at Chapel Hill, nil."

"I thought you were a Dukie," I said, having heard that he was chairman of the Neurology Department there at close to the same time I was in graduate school at Duke.

"I am, but you caan't"—that single word gave away his Boston upbringing—"beat Carolina in the Dean Dome."

"All right," I said. I decided to save the rest of my questions for later. I was satisfied that the man was real, not just a doctor, and that he would treat me as a real person, not as a disease.

"What are we going to do about me?" I said.

We were about to start a series of tests, the results of which would be reviewed by the team, including Joan and me and Dr. Appel, in the morning. On that first day, I was to have a physical exam, chest x-rays, a pulmonary functions test, a spinal tap, blood samples (twenty-five different vials), urinalysis, an EKG, and a repeat of the dreaded EMG and its incessant needles.

A spinal tap was not on my list of things to look forward to. Still, for sheer fright power, it couldn't compete with the EMG. That power was in the hands of a young doctor whose name should go down in the annals of modern medical miracles. Alone among all the stories I have now heard from hundreds of ALS patients, young Dr. Tiwari managed to administer the EMG, chatting with me the whole time, without a single moment of pain. Not one. "It doesn't have to hurt," she said.

When she finished, she said that the chief of the EMG lab would be coming in to check her work. The chief took a more classic approach. He came into the room, picked up the needle, and jabbed it painfully into my arm, then pulled it out and quickly jabbed it in again. He never spoke to me, never even made eye contact. After eight or ten jabs in the arm, he started on my leg.

I felt like a character in some Edgar Allan Poe story; it seemed I was about to be embalmed alive by an unthinking morgue technician. I wondered how he would react if I sat up suddenly and yelled, "Stop! I'm alive!" But I didn't say anything because he was grading Dr. Tiwari—and because he still had the needle. I desperately wanted Dr. Tiwari to tell him that it didn't have to hurt, but that is not how medical schools operate.

As Joan and I headed out to supper that night, we felt thoroughly examined. We had completed in one day all the tests that had taken over a month at home, tests that take more than a year for many ALS patients without access to a comprehensive clinic. And we had met a team of people who, with the single exception of the morgue technician in the EMG lab, had seemed confident and caring. We were ready to attack The Physiatrist's Guide to Real Food in Houston.

Goode Company Barbecue was an inconspicuously plain place on a portion of Kirby Drive dominated by the neon lights of fast-food franchises and small strip shopping centers. If we had not known where to look, we would not have noticed it— a small cinder-block building with cords of mesquite firewood stacked out front. A simple tin-roofed shed ran along the side of the building, sheltering long rows of rough tables and benches. Texas as it was.

Inside, in a single small, dark room, the customers—grizzled men and women in jeans and scuffed boots, stirred in with people in rumpled hospital greens and an occasional suit—simmered in the rich aromas of the mesquite fire and barbecued meat. The line wound among the few forlorn and generally empty indoor tables, past a dusty buffalo head, a stuffed armadillo, and a gigantic leathery Longhorn cow, past iceboxes of bock and blond Shiner beer, to the cafeteria line of offerings: beef brisket, duck, wild turkey, Austin-baked beans, jambalaya, jalapeño bread, and the world's best pecan pie.

Written across the back of the black T-shirts worn by the staff and also in large letters on the wall of the building was this:

YOU MIGHT GIVE SOME SERIOUS THOUGHT
TO THANKING YOUR LUCKY STARS
THAT YOU'RE IN TEXAS.

As Joan and I sipped our first-ever Shiner Bock, we talked about the medical team we had found in Houston. We agreed with the sentiment on the wall.

First thing Tuesday morning, Dr. Appel and his entourage crowded into our room at Methodist Hospital, forming a dense semicircle around the bed on which I sat. All eyes were on the senior resident, a young woman, who began reporting what was in the folder she was holding. All eyes except mine, that is. I was watching the face of Stanley Appel, looking for clues as to the meaning of the report. Some of it I understood. Some of it I did not. In that latter category, Appel's face was not helpful. The woolly worm eyebrows remained inscrutably at rest.

When the resident mentioned severe fasciculations in my tongue, the woolly worms jumped as if they'd been hit by a cattle prod. Dr. Appel moved toward me as the resident and her peers shrank back toward the walls of the room. He grabbed my chin and opened my mouth. "You're wrong," he said to the resident, then stepped back into his place in the semicircle, where he remained until she finished the report.

"What we have learned," Dr. Appel then said to Joan and me, "is consistent with a diagnosis of ALS, although the fasciculations in your tongue are nothing and your breathing is super-good. What we would like to do now is to get your permission for a procedure that will confirm the diagnosis beyond a doubt or let us know that the problem is something other than what we think. Then we will know how to proceed with a program for your care. You will need to sign a consent form for a muscle biopsy."

I spent the remainder of that Tuesday morning undergoing a thorough pulmonary exam and a battery of psychological tests.

On Tuesday afternoon, I wasn't so sure about the role of my lucky stars in bringing me to Texas. The muscle biopsy, I'd been told before I left home, was another one of those things that "they do with a needle." I was a little surprised when the doctor began bathing and then shaving a wide area of my thigh. "We'll make the incision right here," he said.

Incision? I was certain the consent form had not mentioned an incision.

"You're going to feel this," the doctor said. "I'm going to snip a bit of the live muscle tissue. I'm sorry that I cannot use Novocaine, but that would kill the tissue."

Whatever happened to gas?

"You'll feel the snip," he said.

He wasn't kidding.

"Now, we'll do that one more time," he said.

"I only signed one consent form," I protested.

Not a sound from him. *Snip.*

As he was sewing me up, he said, "Don't put any weight on this leg for twenty-four hours. Then walk only with assistance for a couple of days. No hard exercise for two weeks."

"We're having dinner with Peg Pearce tonight," I said. "I haven't seen her since high school." I realized the doctor had no reason to know how good looking Peg Pearce was in high school, but still . . . "When Peg sees me, I'm going to be standing up for a hug."

"You won't be able to stand on that leg," he said. "Just show her your scar." He smiled for the first time. "She'll be impressed."

When Peg and her husband arrived at the motor entrance to the Marriott, Joan helped me stand up. It was worth it. What a hug!

For dinner, they selected Pasquale's, a "casually elegant neighborhood trattoria." They seemed pleased that I had heard of it. It had been recommended by my physiatrist.

The next morning was our final meeting with Dr. Appel. He came in looking into a fat folder of documentation. He was followed by his usual cohort of medical students, but this time, he was also accompanied by some of the other people we had seen in the last few days—the nutritionist, a psychologist, a physical therapist, an occupational therapist, a social worker, and others. It was quite a crowd.

"We now know with certainty," he said to me and to the room, "that what we are dealing with here is in fact ALS."

I do not recall that I had any particular emotional response to his announcement, other than interest in what our team had discovered. Everyone else in the room seemed interested, too. He showed Joan and me and some of the others the photos made from slides of muscle tissue taken—alive—from the leg in which there had not been a single twitch or any sign of weakness. "These cells here," he said, "are what healthy cells look like. These," he said as he pointed to a different place, "show the result of nerve cell death typical in ALS." Carefully, he reviewed the results of all the tests. He appeared to be doing this for instructional purposes directed to his students.

"We cannot predict the course of the disease in any individual," he said to me. "We do know something about statistical experience. About 10 percent of patients die in the first year of the disease. We know you're not in that group. Another 70 percent die in two to five years. Your age, your attitude, your general fitness, and the slight symptoms you have would argue against your being in that group. Beyond that, we really cannot know."

Then he asked if Joan or I had questions for him or anyone in the room.

"Are you familiar with Norman Cousins's book on psycho-neuro-immunology?" I pointed to the book with the prescription for love, hope, faith, joy, laughter, and so on.

Appel glanced at it. "My favorite subject," he said. "He's writing about immune system diseases, and ALS is not an immune system problem. Still, the principles apply. I can't give you any scientific proof, but I can tell you from observation over a twenty-year period: people who feel good about themselves will do better with this disease than people who don't, people who have friends will do better than people who don't, people who resist will do better than people who don't.

"Look," he said, "you already know how little we know about this disease, even though we know as much as anyone in the world. Before you leave here, I want to be certain that you know something else." He spoke very slowly and deliberately. "We do not know what is possible."

We do not know what is possible. I felt liberated by that uncertainty. Instead of focusing on a hopeless death sentence, we would start out on a quest for the possible.

Dr. Appel told us to go home and marshal all our resources to resist the disease. "You don't need to worry about things that haven't happened, about disabilities you don't have. Leave your strategic thinking at the bank. In your personal life, take every day as it comes and make it as good as you can. Your job is to be as healthy as you can be in the day at hand."

I felt as if I should be taking notes, but I doubted I would ever forget the substance of this lecture: Break this overwhelming problem into bite-sized daily chunks and deal with them one at a time. It seemed doable.

"Your friends," my stern physician-counselor added, "are extremely important to your health, but they will need encouragement from you. You will have to help them know how to help you."

I did not think my friends would be much of a problem. They had been trained by Bob Stone.

"We are dealing with two different things here," Dr. Appel explained. "You have the disease, and you have the diagnosis. The diagnosis has caused severe psychological trauma in you, which has led to depression. We know how to cure that. Let's work on that, and then we'll work on the disease." There was complete silence in the room.

"You have ALS," he said. "There's no denying it. But everything that was true about you before you had ALS is still true. Let's put all that to work resisting the disease."

"I'll make a deal," I said to the group crowding the room. "If you all will give me world-class care, I promise you I will be a world-class patient."

◦◊◦

All the way to Houston, Joe and Joan kept thinking of names that should have been on that Thanksgiving letter list. At least it had been delivered to some of the people whose lives touched theirs, and they believed the ones who got it would share it with the ones who didn't. Joe and Joan were certain their friends would continue to want that touch, even from a man diagnosed as dying. Their faith would not let them believe otherwise.

Joe's faith resides somewhere at the core of his being, deeper even than his devotion to the Presbyterian Church. But then faith is to churches as mustangs are to corrals. For some of us, our faith keeps jumping out of whatever house of worship it finds itself in and runs free and wild, surviving on jimson weed, dodging rattlesnakes and rock slides. Joe's faith, on the other hand, had been well nourished and curried all his Protestant life. Born in a Presbyterian manse, the third son of a preacher-man, Joe knew from a very early age where he was supposed to look for God. And he grew up finding God everywhere. Today, as one of his friends, Velva Woollen, puts it, "Joe's faith is like Joe's leg."

So Joe and Joan changed "as fate would have it" to "as faith would have it," and thereby began reconstructing their life. They called on friends and family to rally around them as a community of faith, counting on them to provide down-to-earth proof of God's love. "A good hug," Joe wrote them, "is great theology!"

Hard-hit by the ALS diagnosis, his sister-in-law Dottie Martin took the Thanksgiving letter as gospel. "We talked about it and thought about it all the time. You couldn't not think of this disease. It was the only thing on our minds," Jim Martin's wife remembered.

By the time she got the letter, Dottie had known about the diagnosis for weeks, but she realized that many others would be only just learning about it. "People were to get that letter while Joe and Joan were in Houston, so that by the time they got back, most of Joe's best friends would have the news. I couldn't think of anything worse than having to go through the whole story anytime you ran into somebody, or every time people dropped in. Over and over and over."

Dottie decided it would be a good idea for Joe to face his support group en masse, at a party. She enlisted two co-conspirators, Marilyn Svenson and Susan Abbott, then recruited Nancy Dry from Joe's office. About seventy telephone calls later, they had their party organized for December 1, the very day Joe and Joan were scheduled to return from the Houston clinic, which happened to coincide with Joe's fifty-fourth birthday. Nearly everyone they called wanted to be there for Joe.

Dottie got her son, Jim Jr., to design a T-shirt and banner. Jim Jr. took his inspiration from Joe's letter.

More than a hundred people showed up for the party, which kicked off right in Joe and Joan's front yard as they drove in from the airport. Joe was still in pain from his muscle biopsy, but seeing that enormous demonstration of support made the hurt go away. He stood for hours, hugging and holding hands, talking and listening and eating birthday cake. Maybe, to modify Velva Woollen's expression, Joe wasn't standing on his leg but on faith.

What Dottie Martin and her friends did for Joe was no more than any of us can do for any person in our life who is hurt seemingly beyond help. To be a friend is to take action, to justify faith, to reinforce hope. That, as Joe discovered, is precisely what friends are for.

Chapter Four

N EVER ONCE IN MY LIFE did my father laugh or flinch at my questions, not even in elementary school when I asked him about sex—asked not because I was remotely interested but just to prove to a bunch of other third-grade boys that I could ask my father absolutely anything.

When I was thirty-two, I asked him about eternal life for the same reason I asked my third-grade question about sex: I had no immediate prospects, but I wondered how he would handle the question. I wish now that I had just asked the question straight up, but I prefaced it—prefaced it in one of those ways that can make even adult children insufferable. "You're seventy years old, Pop, and you've been preaching for a long time. What do you really think about eternal life?"

He did not rush, and neither did he flinch. He looked at his hands and said quietly, "I think I will know about that when I need to know." Then, looking me in the eye, he added, "Right now, I know everything I need to know about how to live my life."

Eight years later, in 1980, the question became more timely but harder to ask. At seventy-eight, he was diagnosed with prostate cancer, which had metastasized to his bones. Although he became frail, he kept preaching regularly until the month of his eightieth birthday, which was also the month he died. As I watched him move through his ordeal with cancer—surgeries, pain, weakness—I did not bring up the subject of eternal life again. But I watched, and I listened. I never saw or heard anything that was inconsistent with what he had told me, not to his dying day. To the very end, he didn't allow the power of the cancer to impair his ministry or his life.

He and my mother celebrated Christmas 1982 with all four sons and their wives and an even dozen grandchildren. It was clear to everyone that Pop was playing his role, wearing a tie of his mother's Morrison tartan, telling stories, laughing, hugging everyone, resisting the pain and weakness caused by the cancer, resisting any negative effect on his life. But it was clear to me that he was not resisting death itself. Trusting in what he called "the providence of a sovereign God" in every aspect of life, including death, he had no anxiety, no fear.

On the day after Christmas, in what proved to be the last week of his life, I went to wake him from a nap. He smiled at me and said, "You know, sometimes you think that if no one came to wake you up, you just wouldn't wake up, and that would be all right."

"You're not letting Mama blame me for that," I said. "She's

expecting you in the dining room in fifteen minutes. Get up."

My mother had no less a belief than Pop in the sovereignty of God, but she did not hold that any such concept absolved her from personal responsibility for outcomes. She was not exactly a revolutionary in the orderly kingdom of God, but she expected her opinions to be taken into account.

On New Year's Eve, as I was driving her home from the hospital, where we had finally persuaded the doctors to turn off the life-support equipment, I tried to reassure her: "We've done everything we can, Mama. Now, it's up to Pop and God."

"I suppose," she said very firmly, "but I would like to talk to both of them one more time, just to be sure they're not making some terrible mistake."

With my own mortality at stake twelve years later, I wanted one of those conversations, too. My mind was pounding me with questions. *What exactly is happening to me? And what in the world am I supposed to do about it?* I carried on with my life, I went to work and to workouts, I showed up at parties and civic events, I even felt okay at times, a lot of times. But the questions kept pounding. The diagnosis was never not on my mind.

Going to church should have been the easiest part of every week, and the most comforting. But it was actually the hardest and most challenging. There, I could not even pretend to be thinking of something else. *What is happening to me? What am I supposed to do about it?* There, where I expected to find answers, I had to face the fact that I didn't have any.

I found it fairly easy to control my emotions as I cheered up other people who were saddened by my diagnosis. But try as I might, I had no control in church. My emotions were blown back and forth by constant surprises. Normally, the number of surprises in a Presbyterian worship service is somewhere between few and none. Ditto for emotional outbursts, which are even rarer. So I was unprepared for the degree to which this turn of events in my life made once-familiar and comfortable things in corporate worship seem suddenly very personal and very unsettling.

"The Church's One Foundation" is a perfectly innocuous hymn—a little embarrassing, maybe, in its use of drippy bridal imagery, but so familiar that most people can sing it in good faith without giving the words a second thought. I had noticed, but never stopped to wonder about, the line claiming that the church on earth has—hath—"mystic sweet communion with those whose rest is won." Up to now, I had sung that line as a survivor. Now, I heard it as one whose "rest" was about to be won, like it or not.

But the hymn that really threw me for a loop was one our minister chose to reinforce his nearly constant theme of the sovereignty of God. To match the sturdy music of a Welsh hymn tune, the writer had pulled out all the rhetorical stops. "Immortal, invisible, God only wise," we sang, "In light inaccessible hid from our eyes." This was music that called for timpani. And hoofbeats. And good posture.

And then came the line, "We wither and perish, but nought changeth Thee."

Wither and perish? That was the answer to question number one: *What is happening to me?* Under even the best-case scenario, a person with Lou Gehrig's disease will wither and perish. Precisely that: wither, and then perish. That was what was happening to me. I stopped singing while "wither and perish" still echoed, and I stuck a handkerchief in my mouth to muffle any other sound.

So what about question number two: *What am I supposed to do about it?*

I was preprogrammed to be as skeptical about faith healing as I was about the miracle cures that were for sale everywhere I looked. When I heard that Terri Huntley and Kay Simpson, friends of mine and close friends of Joan's, were attending a weekly "service of prayer for healing" at Christ Episcopal Church—or, as they prefer it, Christ Church (Episcopal), as if maybe we won't notice the parenthetical whisper—my skepticism was reinforced by my genetically transmitted bias against Anglicans. (Those people burned us out of our cottages in Scotland 250 years ago, then ran us out of South Carolina before we could mount an effective revolution against their king. Given enough time, I could get over it. But in 1995, I was still ticked.)

Coming to grips with the disease that took out Lou Gehrig, "the Iron Man of Baseball," I was in no position to be proud. Besides, I wanted to be nice to Terri and Kay. So I folded my Calvinist cloak, shoved it with some difficulty into the closet, and went over to Christ Church (Episcopal) on a Wednesday at ten in the morning. I did not tell anyone I was going.

We met in a small and beautifully paneled chapel that might credibly have been lifted from an elegant eighteenth-century English palace. Terri and Kay were in the front pew, so there I sat, in plain view of everybody. And *sat* is precisely what I did. When they stood for the Gospel (we don't do that), I sat. When they knelt for prayer (we don't do that), I sat. Occasionally, they sat, too. Then I felt really uncomfortable.

The service was presided over by Henry Parsley, then the rector of Christ Church. Henry was a friend and perhaps the gentlest man in all creation. He led us through the *Book of Common Prayer*, his commentary and helpful reference to page numbers overcoming my fear of opening the thing (we don't do that). I was the only person I could see who did not turn to the correct page before Henry announced it. I do not know if he did that for me or if he always made the book and the service seem so accessible.

As I followed the prayers in the book, I found them to be beautiful, genuine, and surprisingly personal. At one point, where a blank line followed a petition for healing and comfort, Henry pulled out a list and began reading names of actual people. (We don't do that. My church is so starkly Presbyterian, so oriented to orderliness, that we pray for people only in categories, preferably alphabetized by the nature of their need: "[a] For all those who are Alone, [b] for all those who are giving Birth, [c] for all those who have Cancer, [d] for all those who have Dozed off," and so on. We could pray for people with ALS, but first a committee would have to rule on whether it would fall properly under *A*, for amyotrophic, or under *L*, for Lou.)

Henry read only the first names of those in need of healing and comfort, but I recognized several neighbors and friends among them. I certainly recognized "Joe." And "Joan," whose tenure as a teacher at Christ Church's kindergarten actually made her senior to Henry on the staff. Joan was no less in need of healing than I, and these Episcopalians were praying for both of us, by name, every Wednesday.

During Henry's homily, I performed an attitude adjustment on myself. The reason my grandparents stood with heads bowed for prayer, after all, was that they considered it to be a properly humble posture in the presence of God. And if the reason my father's congregation sat for prayer had something to do with the length of his prayers, the members were at least also respect-ful of a properly humble posture in the presence of God. There was nothing remotely humble about my posture as I sat—insis-tently sat—in the presence of these Episcopalians, and I repented.

Before the sacraments were served, Henry Parsley explained that people who wanted to participate in prayers for healing, including anointing with oil (we don't do that, but I was in too far to back out now), should just cross their arms in front of them so he would know. Terri leaned toward me and whispered, "He will ask if there is anyone in particular you want to pray for."

So I knelt at the altar rail between Terri and Kay. I heard Terri tell Henry that she wanted him "to pray for my friend Joe," and he did.

It was then my turn, and I had no idea about protocol. Should I ask for reciprocal prayer for Terri? What about Kay? Or would I then be obligating Kay to pray for me, too? I settled on a good Presbyterian category. "All those with ALS," I whispered as Henry bent down to me.

What I then heard from gentle Henry was an earnest and heartfelt prayer for "all those with Alice." *With Alice?* I looked up in a panic, but Henry's eyes were closed, and he plowed ahead. "And for Alice," he said. "May they and she know the healing power of God's love." I relaxed. Whoever Alice might be, she and her friends should be feeling better.

Henry took a bit of oil and made a warm cross on my forehead. Then, with his hands on my shoulders, he prayed: "Joe, I lay my hands upon you in the name of the Father, and of the Son, and of the Holy Spirit, beseeching our Lord Jesus Christ to sustain you with his presence, to drive away all sickness of body and spirit, and to give you that victory of life and peace which will enable you to serve him, both now and evermore. Amen."

For a gentle man, Henry had power in his hands. This time, there was no question that he was praying for me, by name and by touch. The strength of his hands reached from my shoulders to my knees. And I felt a peace I had not known.

As I sat again in the more familiar setting of our own Covenant Presbyterian Church, listening to John Rogers explain the sovereignty of God for the umpteenth time, I finally got it. The point of the hymn was not so much "we wither and perish" as "nought changeth Thee." The certain power and presence of a sovereign God will transcend any triumph and any tragedy we may encounter. "And when you fall," John was saying, "you can fall no farther than the arms of a loving God." I felt a *call* settling into my soul as he concluded with a recitation of his favorite text, from Isaiah: "Thus says the Lord, 'Fear not, for I have redeemed you. I have called you by name. You are mine.'"

So that's what the sovereignty of God was all about. And that's what hope was all about—not wishing that something could happen, but knowing that, whatever happens, we are God's. In that assurance, I found the confidence to get on with my life. It freed me from fear of the unknown. It freed me from doubt based on things beyond my understanding. It did not call me to be heroic. Or courageous. Or to look for miraculous cures. It called me only to live my life in reliance on the certain sovereignty of God. That witness, I could make.

And in that witness was the answer to question number two: *What in the world am I supposed to do about it?* "Right now," Pop had said to me twenty-five years earlier when I asked him about eternal life, "I know everything I need to know about how I should live my life." Finally, as I sat in Covenant's majestic Gothic sanctuary listening to John's sermon, and as I focused on my life, I understood what Pop had said. Whatever happened, I would accept life as the providence of a sovereign God, and I would accept the responsibilities that came to me with that providence.

Most medical waiting rooms, by way of contrast, are depressing places not remotely conducive to thinking about life. If you are not truly sick when you get there, you will be by the time the doctor sees you. This is intentional. The doctor does not want to waste time seeing people who feel good. So patients sit quietly in the waiting room, getting worse and trying hard not to make actual eye contact while sizing up everybody else through their peripheral vision. ("Wonder what she's here for?" "I bet that's what I've got." "They probably think I look as bad as they look. Maybe I do.") To give the plan time to work, the doctor probably will not see you at the hour you thought your appointment was scheduled.

Our first visit to a regular patient-care clinic in Houston after my diagnosis was a mind bender. When we walked into the waiting room, we thought we had stumbled into somebody's party. People were talking and laughing, catching up on family news, showing off new gadgets for their wheelchairs, asking each other for tips on dealing with one symptom or another. We were given nametags—in different colors, so people would know which of us was the patient—and a booklet listing all the people participating that day, along with information about their families, jobs, hometowns, and special interests.

Another couple introduced themselves to us before we could find seats. "Rich Carson. My wife, Lorrie." His nametag was blue, same as mine. "This your first clinic?" Rich and Lorrie became informal hosts for us, explaining how the clinic worked and introducing us to other people. "That's James Keller over there talking with somebody new that we don't know. James was diagnosed two years ago. He's a baseball coach at a college in San Antonio. And a runner." The latter fact was fairly obvious; Keller was wearing shorts and had really strong-looking legs. I tried not to stare, but it was hard to believe he had ALS. The guy he was talking to was bigger, older (maybe my age), and also very athletic looking.

Rich introduced us. James Keller shook hands with a very firm grip. The bigger guy he had been talking to was Billy Anderson, a Houston businessman and former NFL player. Billy had been diagnosed the same month I had. He looked at his booklet as we chatted with James about running.

"You're from Charlotte," Billy Anderson said, looking up from the page containing my name and background. "You know Roman Gabriel?"

I know Roman Gabriel the way I know Joe Montana and Joe Namath—that is, I know who they are. Roman Gabriel was the All-American from North Carolina State who went on to quarterback the Los Angeles Rams. That's where Billy knew him. They were teammates and friends. Now, Roman Gabriel lives in Charlotte. I didn't know that.

Billy Anderson was pure NFL. And I felt bonded to him by the simple fact that we had been diagnosed at the same time. "Billy Anderson and I have ALS. We are going to deal with this together."

The members of the clinic staff were professional, personable, and encouraging. But it was the social life of the waiting room as much as anything else that made the clinic a place of healing. When we left, we were already looking forward to seeing those people again.

We learned some helpful things right away.

1. We generally liked and often admired other people who had ALS. Being with them always gave us a boost.

2. There was no pattern to the pace or sequence of paralysis in different people. We met a man who had been coming to the clinic for fifteen years. He was unable to walk and to feed himself but still had a marvelous operatic voice. Another could not speak but still played racquetball. There was no reason to anticipate any particular disability that another person might have.

3. No matter what disability a person with ALS might

get, somebody already had it—and had figured out how to handle it.

Through the first spring and summer after my diagnosis, interest began building in the possibility that Cal Ripken, Jr., might break Lou Gehrig's "unbreakable" record of 2,130 consecutive games played. It was a bittersweet prospect for those who had Lou Gehrig's incurable disease. Fifty years after his death, "the Iron Man of Baseball" and "the Pride of the Yankees" still gave a kind of dignity to people whose lives seemed so diminished by the disease that carried his name. Because of Ripken's march on Gehrig's record, Gehrig's disease was getting much-needed public attention.

Gehrig's achievement, hailed in 1939 as "a record that will stand for all time," also came to stand for the courage and perseverance of people with ALS. When the record was eclipsed, part of their psychological support would be taken away. And who knew whether the world would lose interest in their hero and in their illness?

Then Cal Ripken did the classiest thing imaginable. He and his team, the Baltimore Orioles, announced that the record-breaking game, due to come in Baltimore's Camden Yards ballpark against the Angels on September 6, 1995, would be played as a benefit for ALS and would establish the Cal Ripken–Lou Gehrig Fund for ALS Research.

Gene Taylor, an old friend then serving as the president of our bank in Maryland, committed a substantial gift to the fund and invited Joan and me to join him in the company's box. Hugh and Jane McColl were invited, too, but Hugh thought he would forgo the honor of the event and the effort of getting there. Less jaded by an excess of historic events, bank executive Ken Lewis and his wife, Donna, decided immediately that they would go with us—an important thing not just because we like Ken and Donna but because we would certainly then take the bank's plane.

Gene called to tell me that President Clinton would be attending the game and that he would be sitting in the box right next to ours. I reported to Hugh that Gene had finagled tickets for the McColls in the president's box. But Hugh had been there and done that, had sat with the president on other occasions and undoubtedly would again. He thought he'd just stay home. Then I read in the paper that Joe DiMaggio would also be in the president's box. I clipped the article and sent it to Hugh.

When Ken and Donna and Joan and I landed in Baltimore, Hugh McColl was already in the hospitality tent at Camden Yards, scouting out DiMaggio. "Look at this," he said. Out of his pockets came six new baseballs, one for each of his grandchildren, and all intended for Joe DiMaggio's autograph.

While Joan checked out the Maryland crab cakes, I stood watch at the entrance to the tent. I had decided to wear my Yankees baseball cap in honor of Lou Gehrig, and I wanted Joe DiMaggio's autograph on it.

"He's not coming in here," Hugh reported. "But I found out how to get his autograph. Every one costs a thousand-dollar contribution to a children's hospital in Florida." I winced. "It's only money," Hugh said, grinning.

Our seats in the bank's box were right on the front row. Joan was on my right, and Chelsea Clinton was on my immediate left. Next to Chelsea was one of her friends, and next to the friend was a chair labeled for the president. Next to that chair was the vice president. Between Chelsea and me was a bulletproof-glass wall.

I was more aware of that wall than of the president. If anyone took a potshot at the president, I would be the nearest unprotected person. All the Secret Service people were on his side of the wall—the safe side. I bet they hadn't even checked what might happen to bullets that couldn't make it through that wall. Would they stick, fall, or ricochet toward whoever might be sitting next to it, unprotected?

Joan and I had been with Bill Clinton a number of times in small groups before he became president, and we loved his company. I was treasurer of the Southern Growth Policies Board when he was chairman, and we attended a good many meetings together. Joan and I thought he was interesting and fun. He always remembered our names (and everybody else's), even in big crowds. I know there's a skill to that, but I believe that Bill Clinton's memory operates from a genuine interest in people. I thought there was a reasonable chance we would see each other at the game, and I did not want the emotional awkwardness—for me, never mind him—of informing him about my diagnosis in front of a bunch of people. So I wrote him a letter telling him of my condition and saying that we were doing fine with it and that we would wave to him at the game if we were close enough.

Before the game started, all of us in the bank's box identified everybody next door in the president's box. As for their side of the bulletproof glass, the presidential party, including Hugh McColl, paid no attention to anybody or to anything going on in our box. The president, in fact, was not in his seat. He was in the back, by the buffet. I left and went to shop for souvenirs.

I was standing in line at one of the vendor booths when a man wearing a suit approached me. The plastic tube running from his ear to the collar of his coat gave him an air of authority. "The president wants to see you," he said.

When Joan and I were ushered into the back of the presidential box, Hugh said quickly, "DiMaggio's not here. He's in the next box over. Nobody can get in there, but I got two autographs."

Two? I didn't have time to ask whether he had folded at the price of six signed balls or at the audacity of asking for that many.

The president came up the steps from his seat on the front row. He grabbed Joan and me both in a gigantic bear hug. I guess I had not been quite that close to him before. I was surprised at how big he was. "We used to have fun together," he said, speaking over the tops of our heads to the others who were standing around. Then he added, "Back when I had a life."

We chatted a little—about what, I do not know. I was busy trying to decide the propriety of handing him my Yankees cap and my pen for an autograph. "Mr. President," I wanted to say, "would you do me the great favor of going next door and getting Joe DiMaggio to sign my hat?"

When he asked how I was doing with my diagnosis, I told him I was fine. "But now that we've broken Lou Gehrig's record," I said, "it's time to break Lou Gehrig's disease."

During the game, the president was invited to the ESPN broadcasting booth, where he told a huge television audience about meeting a friend at the game who has ALS. He also quoted my line. For months after that, I received reports from people who had heard the president say that he had included ALS on his list of "great challenges still facing us."

When the game reached the fifth inning and Ripken's record became official, the contest was interrupted by a genuine ovation for the good guy who now stood alone at 2,131 consecutive baseball games played. The ovation went on so long that it might have set a record itself. At one point, I looked over to the presidential box. The president, turned around and bending over the back of his seat, was signing Hugh McColl's four remaining baseballs—bargains, presumably, compared with DiMaggio's autograph.

Back at home, we discovered that Jim had heard the president's remarks on ESPN and had recorded the whole game. Others had heard, too, and asked if he was talking about us.

That kind of attention, unusual for ALS, made me change my mind about letting the newspaper do a story about my diagnosis. I had declined for months, thinking that I wanted to preserve my privacy and that I didn't want to become known as "the guy with ALS." But the president had shown me the value of exposure and the benefit of knowing that he cared. I decided that I should share that with other ALS patients and families through the newspaper.

The story was given to Karen Garloch on the health beat, who wrote a remarkably broad story that went beyond the medical. It ran on page 1 with a color photo of Joan and me enveloped in Bill Clinton's bear hug. The headline read, "A Good Hug Is Great Theology." The headline on the continuation of the story on an inside page was even better: "It Is Possible to Have Hope."

The article generated a ton of mail to be answered. Most rewarding was word from ALS patients I had never met, who told me they felt less isolated by the disease because they now knew someone who shared it with them.

The *Leader* newspaper then did a story that ran on page 1 under a huge and audacious headline: "Martin Takes on ALS." The privacy of my diagnosis, compromised already by my letter to our friends, was completely shot. Now, the whole community would be watching to see how I handled the disease.

As I began to work with Joe, I found myself needing the truth about my friend's illness. What was going on in Joe's body? It helped me not a whit to know that it was the same thing that had gone on in Lou Gehrig's body. I couldn't remember Gary Cooper twitching—or fasciculating—as he stood in his knickers in the center of Yankee Stadium, hat in hand, folks sobbing all around him. So I decided to begin my search for knowledge just where Joe had begun, with the symptoms he observed. I looked up fasciculation.

In imperial Rome, the fasces *was a symbol of authority, a bundle of rods bound together around an ax handle, the blade of the ax protruding. "United, we will slay you," the Romans advertised on their coins, flags, and shields. In anatomy, a* fasciculus *is a bundle of nerve fibers having common functions and connections. Disunited, they will slay you.*

A fasciculation *is a jumping or twitching of the muscle tissue to*

which these *fasciculi are attached. Often, as in Joe's case, this is the first
sign that the nerve fibers are having their signals from the brain interrupted. The fibers start jumping like an electrical cable that has been
pulled from its mooring in a hurricane and lies flopping and sparking
on the asphalt. And since the brain actually transmits its messages as
wavelike progressions of chemical and electrical impulses, the image is
not far from the reality.*

The immediate cause of Joe's fasciculations was a degeneration of
lower motor neurons. Motor neurons are the nerve cells that carry the
"move it now" impulses from our spinal cord to our muscles. In Joe's
body, neurons started blowing out like overexcited fuses. All this is the
amyotrophic *part of amyotrophic lateral sclerosis.* A–myo–trophic *means*
no–muscle–nourishment.

Then there are the upper motor neurons, *which transmit the
brain's "move it now" message over the first half of the nerve circuit,
from the brain to the spinal cord, specifically to the lateral (side) part of
the spinal cord. In ALS, these nerve cells blow out, too, hence the second
part of the disease's name,* lateral. *The spinal cord, by the way, begins at
the brain's medulla oblongata, which is what we know as the brain stem
and what neurologists call the bulbar region, because it is bulb shaped.*

When they take off from the bulbar region, "move it now" signals
travel along the cord through the spinal canal, formed by the openings in
the successive vertebrae. As the upper motor neurons start to go, a person
suffers stiffness, muscle cramping, and weakness. If these are the first
fuses to blow out, the early signs of ALS will be difficulties with walking or manual dexterity. If the upper motor neurons specifically located
in the bulbar region degenerate first, the early symptoms may involve*

problems with speaking or swallowing.

When the lateral part of the spinal cord begins to harden, that is sclerosis, the third part of the disease's name. There are other diseases, such as progressive bulbar palsy and primary lateral sclerosis, that imitate ALS, but none of these does such complete damage as Joe's body has endured. No matter which symptoms manifest themselves in the early stages, the true ALS patient eventually will experience them all. Almost every muscle we know as voluntary, or moved at will, will be affected by ALS sooner or later. Among the few exceptions in most ALS patients are the voluntary muscles that move the eyes, and this is of enormous importance in surviving.

None of Joe's involuntary muscles is likely to be affected by the motor neuron loss. Nor are the nerves that carry impulses in the opposite direction—namely, his senses. Joe can still feel a touch or a hug or a needle stab, and he can still see and hear and smell. ALS does not take away one's bladder or bowel functions or diminish one's sexuality. ALS is not itself the cause of physical pain. However, a person with ALS faces the ultimate loss of respiratory muscles; one day, or one night, the breathing will stop.

Of course, that much is true for all of us. The difference is that, at some point between diagnosis and final breath, people with ALS are likely to become fully functioning minds with immovable bodies. From the moment they understand their disease, they must put their minds to work on survival skills. That's why the eyes are so important: even with the worst damage ALS can do, the eyes remain the mind's outlet to the world.

To help people with ALS, there were in 1994 some twenty comprehensive research and patient-care clinics in the United States. Some were

Both Erskine, an invest-
~~:~~e, and his wife, Crandall,
~~.~~ from philanthropic fami-
~~r~~skine Bowles took a call

Mac McDonald, Erskine
Derick Close listened to
challenge to Linda Street
if your family will match

~~:~~e next meeting, she raised
~~s~~aid, "and we don't think
~~r~~ family will match it."

~~:~~e both wearing that deer-
"We'll have to talk to
family who can keep up

~~:~~ho refused to apply pres-
the NationsBank Foun-
~~:~~es had committed so far.
~~J~~oe and Jim had lined up
~~C~~enter.

~~e~~longs to his brother. "Jim
~~p~~roposal," he told me. "I
~~:~~as I saw the possibility
it with or without me. I

supported by the ALS Association, some were supported by the Muscular Dystrophy Association—the Jerry Lewis Telethon people—and a few were sponsored jointly. At the time of Joe's diagnosis, none of these clinics was in the southeastern United States, near his base of operations in Charlotte, North Carolina. The MDA and ALSA "comprehensive" clinics have a commitment to patient care and to helping people learn to manage life with the disease; they also search for clues to treatments and cures. Additional research goes on in hundreds of academic centers and pharmaceutical companies.

ALS could be caused by a virus, as is polio. It could be related to some genetic flaw (although only about 5 percent of cases are considered hereditary) that disrupts the structural integrity of motor neurons. A good bit of the research is focused on some of the complex chemical compounds assembled in the body's cellular laboratories. In these tiny chemical labs, a few basic building blocks—such as oxygen, carbon, hydrogen, nitrogen, phosphorous, and calcium—are juggled and permutated into nearly as many compounds as the sky has stars. These are the compounds that long ago enabled humankind to crawl out of the primordial soup and start becoming all that we can be.

Somewhere in there are the clues that researchers will find someday. But in 1994, they were still clueless. What they were certain of were the statistics. Out of every hundred thousand people born, between one and two will develop ALS, usually between the ages of fifty-three and fifty-seven. Roughly two out of every three patients are male.

Just a month before Joe's diagnosis, an ALS support group was formed in Charlotte by Brenda Craig and Anita Drobka (both of whose families had been touched by ALS) and Jeri-Ann Cheswick, a nurse and health administrator who had helped Anita's husband, Tom, through

his final months with the illness. Whatever their hopes for the grou
unlikely they could have imagined the level of support that woul
out of it.

Jim Martin went with Joe and Joan to support-group meetings,
they met people who had no means of flying to Houston every
three months, people who could not afford high-end motorized
people who would never have eye-powered computers to link th
the world, people who could not pay a personal staff to enable th
live every moment to its fullest. But most importantly, these friend
hundreds of other people like them had no means of obtaining th
of specialists who understood Lou Gehrig's disease. The best ma
them had was doctors who could let them know when it was ti
consider life support and living wills.

In early 1996, Jim decided to see what it would take to s
clinic in Charlotte that would provide some of what Stan Appel's
provided in Houston. He and Dottie and Joe and Joan had bee
vited to Puerto Vallarta, Mexico, by Joan's sister and brother-ir
Katherine and Larry Youngblood. On the way home, Jim and I
paid a visit to the Houston center to find out what it would cos
who might help pay for it. They came back with the realization t
was going to take a bundle of money and that they would be wis
to expect help from national organizations and foundations. Wh
money they needed would have to be raised locally.

It did not hurt that Jim, a former governor and congressman
now vice president of research at the region's largest hospital net
Carolinas Medical Center. Jim realized that an ALS treatment fa
would not be a financially attractive enterprise for a hospital, espec

an officer of Duke Power, had died with ALS
ment banker with a commitment to public ser
CEO of Springs Mills textile company, cam
lies. Before he could get out of Washington,
from Jim Martin about the clinic.

At a meeting in Charlotte, Linda and
and Crandall Bowles, and Crandall's brothe
Jim and Joe's request. Erskine Bowles put th
McDonald: "My family will give $100,000
it."

Linda went away to think about it. At t
Bowles's bet. "My family discussed it," she
that's enough. We'll put up $500,000 if yo

"Done," said Erskine.

Then they turned to Jim and Joe, who w
in-the-headlights look. Jim spoke up quickl
Hugh McColl. He's the only person in our
with you."

The group called on Hugh (without Joe,
sure on his friend and employer). McColl sai
dation would match what each of the fami
After what amounted to three telephone calls,
exactly $1.5 million for the Carolinas ALS

Joe is adamant that the credit for all this
had the idea, developed the concept and the
was reluctant at first, then more enthusiasti
taking shape and saw that he was going to

agreed to go along, even to help. I agreed to give the proposal a personal face and to make the problem visible. A classic case of becoming the leader of a parade that is already under way!"

But having Joe in front of the parade was like blowing up a giant Macy's balloon to lead a high-school band. The group decided to set its sights higher. "If we could raise $3 million," Jim said, "then the interest would generate enough cash to guarantee the ongoing operation of the center."

During the next year, the community became aware of the Martin brothers' mission, and local foundations began to ante up. They heard from other ALS patients and their families. One of the city's most successful trade shows, the Southern Spring Show, offered to make the nascent center the beneficiary of its February 1998 opening-night program. CEO Joan Zimmerman thought the show might raise as much as $50,000, but after the growing list of committed individuals put out the word, nearly three thousand people showed up for preview night, raising more than $135,000 for the Carolinas ALS Center Endowment.

In May 1998, the Carolinas Neuromuscular/ALS Center opened its doors, one month ahead of schedule. It was headed by Dr. Jeffrey Rosenfeld, an energetic, thoughtful, and thought-provoking physician recruited from Emory University.

Dr. Rosenfeld was a bit awed at the way it happened and the speed at which it came together. "Most of the time, a medical center identifies a need in the community, or there is someone with an interest, and they go and look for donors, and the donors rise to the need," he said. "In this case, donors came to the medical center and said, 'Create this here.' And the medical center said yes. That was new for me."

Less than six months after it opened, the center began helping to write the history of beating Lou Gehrig's disease by conducting groundbreaking clinical trials on ALS treatments. That brought unexpected national media attention. By the end of 1998, calls for help were coming in from as far away as Turkey. One CBS News report swamped the center's call center with more than four hundred patient inquiries from Alaska, California, Florida, Louisiana, Maine, Minnesota, Missouri, and North Dakota.

The dark-eyed, dark-haired young doctor in the white lab coat was overwhelmed by the response. "We have learned about patients who were so pleased, or 'shocked,' as they say, about the quality of what they saw here, from the TV report, that they put announcements out on the Internet: 'I can't believe what a resource we just stumbled on.' I've seen several of those. So the word is out.

"Joe and Jim set the wheels in motion," continued Dr. Rosenfeld, "and the wheel was big enough. I'd say that it was a bigger wheel than I had ever turned before—bigger than any wheel I had even seen before. And it was exciting. It still is exciting."

Dr. Rosenfeld is optimistic that eventually a cure will be found for amyotrophic lateral sclerosis. "I do think that. I think that we will first see a way to change the course of the disease, and then we will see a cure. That's in my most optimistic moments. If in my lifetime I found a way to stall the disease, that would be enough. . . . That would be enough."

Chapter   Five

I N ONE OF LIFE'S MIND–BENDING MOMENTS, Joan and I became grandparents. Joe B. and Jodi presented us with Joseph Bacon Martin *V*! (Someday, someone will break that chain, but it probably won't be someone who ever knew my mother.) We were excited, more than ready to claim grandparenthood, but there were twinges of sadness, too.

Joseph's other grandfather, Alan Bond, had died just a month earlier. Alan was diagnosed with multiple sclerosis not long after his marriage to his college sweetheart. He and Lynn became profiles in the simple courage of living—pursuing careers, maintaining friendships, raising a family, continuing to be themselves right on through Alan's near-total paralysis. When Joseph was born, I hoped he would someday be able to understand the joy he gave his grandfather Bond just by providing the anticipation of life in Alan's final days. And I hoped I would somehow find a way to play a credible role as grandfather.

At the office, Chuck Cooley and I spent hours figuring out how to hold life and work together around the ALS diagnosis. After recruiting me to the company in 1973, Chuck had persevered as my friend and coach. I had learned to trust him completely.

"How long do you think I could stay here with this disease?" I asked him.

"As long as you can keep your spirits up—and your good humor."

"What if I can't keep up with the work load, can't keep up a reasonable schedule?"

"What's different about that?" he said. "Look, just assume that you have a new job. Your job from here on is to make yourself available to us as much as possible for as long as possible."

So I stayed put. Truth is, I now realized how much I needed the *company* of my company. These were people who trusted each other, who loved winning together. They knew how to build teams and, if need be, how to carry a struggling teammate to the finish line. I hugged them close and took their unbridled corporate confidence into my personal life.

Besides, in Dick Stilley and Lynn Drury and their associates, I had the best corporate affairs team in America. No one outside would notice if I stumbled.

Hugh McColl assigned me to a project in San Antonio, where our bank had gotten behind the efforts of Ernie Cortes and his supported by the ALS Association, some were supported by the Muscular Dystrophy Association—the Jerry Lewis Telethon people—and a few were sponsored jointly. At the time of Joe's diagnosis, none of these clinics was in the southeastern United States, near his base of operations in Charlotte, North Carolina. The MDA and ALSA "comprehensive" clinics have a commitment to patient care and to helping people learn to manage life with the disease; they also search for clues to treatments and cures. Additional research goes on in hundreds of academic centers and pharmaceutical companies.

ALS could be caused by a virus, as is polio. It could be related to some genetic flaw (although only about 5 percent of cases are considered hereditary) that disrupts the structural integrity of motor neurons. A good bit of the research is focused on some of the complex chemical compounds assembled in the body's cellular laboratories. In these tiny chemical labs, a few basic building blocks—such as oxygen, carbon, hydrogen, nitrogen, phosphorous, and calcium—are juggled and permutated into nearly as many compounds as the sky has stars. These are the compounds that long ago enabled humankind to crawl out of the primordial soup and start becoming all that we can be.

Somewhere in there are the clues that researchers will find someday. But in 1994, they were still clueless. What they were certain of were the statistics. Out of every hundred thousand people born, between one and two will develop ALS, usually between the ages of fifty-three and fifty-seven. Roughly two out of every three patients are male.

Just a month before Joe's diagnosis, an ALS support group was formed in Charlotte by Brenda Craig and Anita Drobka (both of whose families had been touched by ALS) and Jeri-Ann Cheswick, a nurse and health administrator who had helped Anita's husband, Tom, through his final months with the illness. Whatever their hopes for the group, it is unlikely they could have imagined the level of support that would grow out of it.

Jim Martin went with Joe and Joan to support-group meetings, where they met people who had no means of flying to Houston every two or three months, people who could not afford high-end motorized chairs, people who would never have eye-powered computers to link them to the world, people who could not pay a personal staff to enable them to live every moment to its fullest. But most importantly, these friends and hundreds of other people like them had no means of obtaining the care of specialists who understood Lou Gehrig's disease. The best many of them had was doctors who could let them know when it was time to consider life support and living wills.

In early 1996, Jim decided to see what it would take to start a clinic in Charlotte that would provide some of what Stan Appel's clinic provided in Houston. He and Dottie and Joe and Joan had been invited to Puerto Vallarta, Mexico, by Joan's sister and brother-in-law, Katherine and Larry Youngblood. On the way home, Jim and Dottie paid a visit to the Houston center to find out what it would cost and who might help pay for it. They came back with the realization that it was going to take a bundle of money and that they would be wise not to expect help from national organizations and foundations. Whatever money they needed would have to be raised locally.

It did not hurt that Jim, a former governor and congressman, was now vice president of research at the region's largest hospital network, Carolinas Medical Center. Jim realized that an ALS treatment facility would not be a financially attractive enterprise for a hospital, especially a *private hospital. "My acquaintance with the budget process had helped me to understand that it would be very difficult to persuade even a public hospital to establish a comprehensive care program for ALS if it was going to lose a lot of money," he said. "We had to first show that we could start a center here, and then go to them. Joe began thinking, 'Well, could we raise $1 million? What would it take to raise $1 million?'"*

Michael Rose, head of the Carolinas Healthcare Foundation, told the Martin brothers that he would be willing to administer their fund, should they get it going. Rose volunteered to help them raise the start-up money as an earmarked endowment and said he would provide matching dollars to help get it started.

But where to turn for private contributions? The most likely sources would be families like theirs who had been touched by the disease. The Martin brothers knew two prominent local families who met that description.

One was the family of Robert "Bobby" Street, who had been one of the Carolinas' preeminent building contractors. In fact, the NationsBank Corporate Center, where Joe worked, was Street's last project before he died from ALS complications. His daughter, Linda Street McDonald, was approachable.

So was the Bowles family. At Camden Yards for Cal Ripken's record-breaking game, Joe had talked with Clinton aide Erskine Bowles, who said he'd like to help Joe in any way possible, once he returned to North Carolina from the White House. The Bowleses had been struck twice by Lou Gehrig's disease. First, Erskine's father, Hargrove "Skipper" Bowles, vice chairman of First Union Bank, then his sister Martha, an officer of Duke Power, had died with ALS. Both Erskine, an investment banker with a commitment to public service, and his wife, Crandall, CEO of Springs Mills textile company, came from philanthropic families. Before he could get out of Washington, Erskine Bowles took a call from Jim Martin about the clinic.

At a meeting in Charlotte, Linda and Mac McDonald, Erskine and Crandall Bowles, and Crandall's brother Derick Close listened to Jim and Joe's request. Erskine Bowles put the challenge to Linda Street McDonald: "My family will give $100,000 if your family will match it."

Linda went away to think about it. At the next meeting, she raised Bowles's bet. "My family discussed it," she said, "and we don't think that's enough. We'll put up $500,000 if your family will match it."

"Done," said Erskine.

Then they turned to Jim and Joe, who were both wearing that deer-in-the-headlights look. Jim spoke up quickly. "We'll have to talk to Hugh McColl. He's the only person in our family who can keep up with you."

The group called on Hugh (without Joe, who refused to apply pressure on his friend and employer). McColl said the NationsBank Foundation would match what each of the families had committed so far. After what amounted to three telephone calls, Joe and Jim had lined up exactly $1.5 million for the Carolinas ALS Center.

Joe is adamant that the credit for all this belongs to his brother. "Jim had the idea, developed the concept and the proposal," he told me. "I was reluctant at first, then more enthusiastic as I saw the possibility taking shape and saw that he was going to do it with or without me. I *agreed to go along, even to help. I agreed to give the proposal a personal face and to make the problem visible. A classic case of becoming the leader of a parade that is already under way!"*

But having Joe in front of the parade was like blowing up a giant Macy's balloon to lead a high-school band. The group decided to set its sights higher. "If we could raise $3 million," Jim said, "then the interest would generate enough cash to guarantee the ongoing operation of the center."

During the next year, the community became aware of the Martin brothers' mission, and local foundations began to ante up. They heard from other ALS patients and their families. One of the city's most successful trade shows, the Southern Spring Show, offered to make the nascent center the beneficiary of its February 1998 opening-night program. CEO Joan Zimmerman thought the show might raise as much as $50,000, but after the growing list of committed individuals put out the word, nearly three thousand people showed up for preview night, raising more than $135,000 for the Carolinas ALS Center Endowment.

In May 1998, the Carolinas Neuromuscular/ALS Center opened its doors, one month ahead of schedule. It was headed by Dr. Jeffrey Rosenfeld, an energetic, thoughtful, and thought-provoking physician recruited from Emory University.

Dr. Rosenfeld was a bit awed at the way it happened and the speed at which it came together. "Most of the time, a medical center identifies a need in the community, or there is someone with an interest, and they go and look for donors, and the donors rise to the need," he said. "In this case, donors came to the medical center and said, 'Create this here.' And the medical center said yes. That was new for me."

Less than six months after it opened, the center began helping to write the history of beating Lou Gehrig's disease by conducting groundbreaking clinical trials on ALS treatments. That brought unexpected national media attention. By the end of 1998, calls for help were coming in from as far away as Turkey. One CBS News report swamped the center's call center with more than four hundred patient inquiries from Alaska, California, Florida, Louisiana, Maine, Minnesota, Missouri, and North Dakota.

The dark-eyed, dark-haired young doctor in the white lab coat was overwhelmed by the response. "We have learned about patients who were so pleased, or 'shocked,' as they say, about the quality of what they saw here, from the TV report, that they put announcements out on the Internet: 'I can't believe what a resource we just stumbled on.' I've seen several of those. So the word is out.

"Joe and Jim set the wheels in motion," continued Dr. Rosenfeld, "and the wheel was big enough. I'd say that it was a bigger wheel than I had ever turned before—bigger than any wheel I had even seen before. And it was exciting. It still is exciting."

Dr. Rosenfeld is optimistic that eventually a cure will be found for amyotrophic lateral sclerosis. "I do think that. I think that we will first see a way to change the course of the disease, and then we will see a cure. That's in my most optimistic moments. If in my lifetime I found a way to stall the disease, that would be enough. . . . That would be enough."

Chapter Five

I N ONE OF LIFE'S MIND–BENDING MOMENTS, Joan and I became grandparents. Joe B. and Jodi presented us with Joseph Bacon Martin *V*! (Someday, someone will break that chain, but it probably won't be someone who ever knew my mother.) We were excited, more than ready to claim grandparenthood, but there were twinges of sadness, too.

Joseph's other grandfather, Alan Bond, had died just a month earlier. Alan was diagnosed with multiple sclerosis not long after his marriage to his college sweetheart. He and Lynn became profiles in the simple courage of living—pursuing careers, maintaining friendships, raising a family, continuing to be themselves right on through Alan's near-total paralysis. When Joseph was born, I hoped he would someday be able to understand the joy he gave his grandfather Bond just by providing the anticipation of life in Alan's final days. And I hoped I would somehow find a way to play a credible role as grandfather.

At the office, Chuck Cooley and I spent hours figuring out how to hold life and work together around the ALS diagnosis. After recruiting me to the company in 1973, Chuck had persevered as my friend and coach. I had learned to trust him completely.

"How long do you think I could stay here with this disease?" I asked him.

"As long as you can keep your spirits up—and your good humor."

"What if I can't keep up with the work load, can't keep up a reasonable schedule?"

"What's different about that?" he said. "Look, just assume that you have a new job. Your job from here on is to make yourself available to us as much as possible for as long as possible."

So I stayed put. Truth is, I now realized how much I needed the *company* of my company. These were people who trusted each other, who loved winning together. They knew how to build teams and, if need be, how to carry a struggling teammate to the finish line. I hugged them close and took their unbridled corporate confidence into my personal life.

Besides, in Dick Stilley and Lynn Drury and their associates, I had the best corporate affairs team in America. No one outside would notice if I stumbled.

Hugh McColl assigned me to a project in San Antonio, where our bank had gotten behind the efforts of Ernie Cortes and his

Industrial Areas Foundation to organize the Hispanic majority. Hugh had met Cortes and, predictably, had given him the impression of big-time support. I was dispatched to resolve the difference between the expectations of Cortes ($1 million plus) and the reality of our budget for San Antonio ($50,000, maybe).

I knew the drill: Hugh's job was to plant dreams; ours was to reap results. It did not matter to him that his job was easier than ours. He kept score on results.

I told Hugh I didn't know if I should get started on what might become a long-term project.

"I don't either," he said. "Just go." Not then or ever did he seem to have a short-term view of my involvement in the company.

The short version of the Ernie Cortes story is that we "compromised" on $500,000 as seed money to expand his program to other markets of ours, with a promise of more if results were achieved. We would eventually exceed not only the San Antonio budget but even Ernie's expectations. His results in stabilizing neighborhoods and increasing home ownership, in demanding city services, in improving schools and school attendance, in providing job training and attracting investments in new jobs would make those markets safer and more profitable for the bank.

The San Antonio experience taught me something. The confession of my diagnosis to Ernie and his associates was intended to let them know that I might not be able to stay the course. They took it instead as an indication of my genuine interest that I would come talk with them despite my illness, and they showed me with their concern over many months that they cared about me personally and were interested in what I had to say. It was the beginning of my recognition of changes—positive changes—in the way people perceived me as I let them know what I was dealing with. And I was happy to have the prayers of the wonderfully tough nuns who were part of the project.

Not long afterward, when a delegation of civic leaders said they wanted to visit with me "about the Urban League," all my defenses went up. The bank's contributions budget had to be protected. And it was not the Urban League's turn.

What they wanted was not money. They wanted me to accept the Whitney M. Young Award at their annual benefit gala. I was stunned. I was also embarrassed to have my contributions to racial justice held up to public scrutiny. I told them I would think about it, but I was seriously worried that they had been blinded by the dire circumstances of my illness. I could see them, with the best of intentions, arriving at the event and making fools of all of us by finding that there wasn't much to be said of the honoree except that he was sick.

I asked Dick Stilley to find out if the Urban League had given any actual thought to this proposal and to determine whether they could make a credible case for giving me the award. His report was convincing, if not exactly a boost to my ego. "They can make a good case," he said, "especially if they combine you and the company." Then he added a stiletto to my balloon: "And if we help." But he also said none of that really mattered. "Giving you the award will be good for them, and they need something good." So I agreed to accept.

I wrote two speeches. One was a safe and perfectly good thank-you that would leave people saying, "Didn't Joe do a good job? And isn't it a shame that he's so ill?" The other, closer to the edge, recognized the hidden racism we all carry with us and would leave people saying, "Did you hear that? Is he losing it, or could he be right? Can we really do something to make a difference?"

The message in the second speech was tough: "The racism that keeps us apart, that keeps us from moving forward, is not the blatant racism of Klansmen and neo-Nazis, but the undisclosed racism that all of us sophisticated social liberals of all stripes and colors carry around in our heads and in our hearts." I tried to apply Norman Cousins's principles as I was applying them to my personal health: (1) Face the truth—don't deny it, but do defy its effect on your life; (2) Construct an environment of love, hope, faith, joy, laughter, festivity, sense of purpose, determination, and will to live together; (3) Break the problem into small and manageable daily chunks, then turn race into a positive force.

I thought the speech was compelling. And really funny. And really risky. People don't talk about race with joy and laughter. We are so accustomed to talking about race in anger and fear and suspicion and frustration that we think we're not being honest if those elements are missing. I was afraid I could be out of touch with reality. I could be losing it. I could make a fool of myself.

I gathered my bank teammates, a mix of men and women, young and old, black and white, native Charlotteans and transplants. They were paid to be in touch with the reality in which we operated, to understand when and how that reality could be changed, and to know when it could not be changed. I gave them both speeches.

During the first one, the safe one, they smiled and nodded.

Fine speech. During the second one, their body language changed. Some fidgeted; some froze. Melba Spencer put her head down on the table so that I could not see her face. Melba is a bright and personable African American with an urban in-your-face self-confidence. I have tremendous respect and great affection for her. I did not know whether I had offended her, dismayed her, or bored her into a coma. When I finished, she looked up, minus the smile that is her hallmark, and said, "You have to give that speech. That message is so important to all of us, and none of us may ever get this good an opportunity to deliver it."

And so The Speech was on. The cost to my group for having me accept their advice: they had to attend the dinner, listen to the speech again, and laugh loudly at all the punch lines.

I still had minimal paralysis in the early fall of 1996, but I told the Urban League that they should have Plan B ready in case I could not attend the spring event. "Plan B is, we give it to you anyway," they said. Posthumously is no doubt what they had in mind, but I let it pass.

My voice was still strong, resonant, clear. I was so happy about my voice that I sang louder than usual at church. I sang in the shower, in the car, anywhere I could. When singing was really inappropriate—as, for example, in the acoustically live basement garage at the bank—I whistled. It proved that my lips worked.

As I was talking about the garden one afternoon, I was surprised that I could not say "daylily." I could say "day" and "lily" separately, but I could not make the rhetorical slide from one to the other. I noticed the same problem with the *l* in "neurologist" and "clinic." My speech was clear if I avoided sounds that were difficult. "Neurologists" became "neuro-types." Going to the "clinic" became a matter of visiting my "Houston medical team." If "daylilies" came up, I changed the subject. Nobody noticed the difference.

Then "daylily" came back. I have no idea why. Maybe the muscle weakness in my tongue that caused the problem was offset by new weakness in the countervailing muscles, so that some equilibrium was restored. Whatever the reason, life became a constant game of Password, with an interesting twist: the rules were subject to change without notice.

Speech pathologists on my Houston medical team showed me how every sound required an incredibly complex sequence of muscle actions. When weakness developed in the mouth or lips or tongue or throat or lungs, the sequence could be thrown off.

There were several ways to deal with the problem. I could slow down and give the weak muscles a chance to get in line. I could practice sounds, maybe while reading aloud to myself, to give my body a chance to find some new way to reproduce the sound I wanted.

More important than all this, they reminded me that the purpose of language was not to speak perfectly but to be understood fully. And they showed me how to use nonverbal resources—such as pauses, shrugs, posture, facial expressions, and, most of all, eyes—to give hearers instant clues to the meaning of what I was saying.

The result was remarkable. I found people watching my eyes intently as I spoke and generally paying no notice when my lips or tongue stumbled over something.

The problem of muscle control was not limited to my voice.

The index finger on my right hand had begun to curl under in December 1995, and I could not extend it. Worse, my ring finger and little finger on that hand had begun to curl also, especially when I held that hand up. My middle finger had the opposite problem; I could not curl it at all. The result: when I waved at people, I would involuntarily give them the finger. I discovered this at the YMCA, where I could see in the mirrors that every time one of the Nautilus machines caused me to raise my arms, I flipped the bird to everyone in the room.

Dr. Appel observed the problem on one of my clinic visits. "Look," he said, "we have two options. Either we amputate that finger or you're going to lose all your friends."

Luckily, as with "daylilies," the finger dilemma righted itself. The middle finger eventually curled like the others.

The occupational therapist in the Houston clinic, a short-story writer who encouraged me to keep writing, had some simple solutions for the problems with my fingers: (1) Put the laptop in my lap, so my arms would remain down and the fingers would relax their curl; and (2) use spring-loaded finger splints that would straighten the fingers after I flexed them to hit the keys.

About the time I had mastered the problem, the index finger returned to service, followed by the others. Now, I could extend them for typing, but I could not flex them to hold a pen. And I could not give anyone the finger even when I wanted to.

At the office, I relied on my left hand to compensate for whatever was wrong with the right hand day to day. I was surprised at how easily the left hand could cover as much or as little of the typewriter keyboard as necessary—and without my having even to think about it, let alone look at the keyboard. My left hand seemed to be saying, "What took you so long to find me?"

Years earlier, my college fraternity brother and friend Bob Bradford had invited me to what became an annual spring fly-fishing trip to his family's place in the Poconos. First, he had to teach me to use a fly rod, which he did by demonstration: "Hold it like this. Bring it back like this." I was so intent on maintaining a count of two for each motion and on moving the rod only from the two o'clock position to ten o'clock that I never noticed that Bob was left-handed. I did everything as he said—"Like this." So I learned to fish left-handed. And so I should not have been surprised that my left hand was ready when called upon.

One thing my left hand could not do was reproduce my signature. It could write legibly enough but could not come close to the bold, round letterforms of *Joe* that I recognized as me. It bugged me. Each time I failed to get it right, I would crumple the paper and slam it on the floor. When Nancy Dry had enough of this, she started stockpiling paper wads on her desk, in view of mine. Every time I tossed a bungled signature in my frustration, I would get hit by a barrage of paper hand grenades from Nancy's desk.

Eventually, Nancy tired of the game and my outbursts. She brought me several old memos I had signed years ago and asked which signatures I liked best. Then she had one reproduced as a rubber stamp so that I could sign my "real name." End of frustration.

I had enough general weakness in my right hand that I began

to use a buttonhook for the buttons on my dress shirts that I could not reach with my left hand. Joan's newly formed "sewing group" took on a project of Joan's design—took it on quite possibly because they needed some rationale for their weekly get-togethers. They removed the buttons from my dress shirts, replaced them with Velcro tabs, and then sewed the buttons on the outside, so the shirts would appear to be buttoned. I was thrilled with the results. Then we sent my dirty shirts to the cleaner, and the steam press melted all the Velcro tabs. I was happy when the sewing group turned to making egg custard for me.

There were other home remedies. I nailed a fingernail clipper to a short piece of two-by-four, so I could use it by pressing the butt of my hand on the lever instead of having to squeeze it between the weak thumb and forefinger of my right hand. I wore a brace on my right wrist, partly to keep that hand from flopping around but mainly as a cosmetic device to indicate that there was something wrong with that arm. I found that such a clue, for some reason, caused people not to look twice at the dangling hand.

What I was learning, when I was not totally exasperated by the ebb and flow of creeping paralysis, was that a progressive disease like ALS is a slow-motion trauma. Either you die a thousand deaths, grieving for every loss, or you recognize that this condition is coming to you in manageable chunks. Despair that prevents you from dealing with any such daily dosage of disability makes the next round harder. Success—or even a good effort—on a daily basis becomes part of the routine of life, and the progress of the disease becomes less disheartening.

Almost always, there is some "fix" close at hand, since any disability is bound to be one that somebody else has had and has already figured out. Me, I enjoyed finding my own solutions—finding them at the hardware store or at a sports shop or on the Internet or, as a last resort, at a medical supply place. Reinventing the wheel, after all, is the only way to share the incredible satisfaction experienced by whoever actually invented the wheel.

By the end of 1996, I was uneasy enough about walking that I tried—and rejected—a cane. I didn't like the looks of it, and I had to lean over in order to put my weight on it. From Bradford's fishing trips to the Poconos, I knew I could do better with a hiking stick, the sort a fisherman uses to steady himself in the stream. At a sports store, I found an incredibly lightweight and strong titanium stick. It had a strap to loop around my wrist for extra steadiness and was enough to help me keep my balance. And it made me stand up straight. It made me look less like Grandma Moses and more like Moses himself.

The problem of maintaining balance ruled out running and bicycling. But I was desperate for fresh-air exercise. Looking on the Internet for a tricycle that would be more sporty than the clunkers that old ladies drive to the grocery store, I kept running into the word *recumbent*. It turned out that there were dozens of models of recumbent tricycles designed not for disabilities but for touring and racing. I found one that was perfect for my abilities. It had a lay-back seat that was easy on my back; the pedals were mounted at a raised angle that increased the force of each push; the steering worked by leaning my body one way or the other (and did not require me to hold handlebars or support any weight on my arms). It was a great machine—and the envy of the neighborhood kids. I could ride for an hour, hit speeds of thirty-five miles per hour, get my heart rate up, and breathe as deeply as I had when I was running. Lying close to the ground as the pavement sped by and leaning into the curves, I felt like I was riding a dry-land luge.

Wearing my aerodynamic helmet and bike gloves, I wheeled into Hugh McColl's driveway to show off my new toy and, to be honest, to show off how cool I looked. He was impressed. "That's perfect," he said. "Of course, your neighbors are going to think you look a little eccentric. But other than that, it's perfect."

Despite all the things we had dealt with, I was still independent at the end of 1996. I was slow—in walking and writing and dressing—and my voice seemed to me to be losing some of its resonance, but I needed very little assistance with anything. I drove, I went anywhere I wanted to on my own, and I had found a way to continue outdoor exercise.

Friends and relatives pitched in with help—sometimes with creative help we would not have asked for. Some tended to the garden when we were away. Others prepared entire dinner parties so we could continue to invite guests to our house. Joan's sister Mary flew down from Minneapolis to give the house a good cleaning. Some people sent inspirational messages, and some sent things to make us laugh; sometimes, they were the same thing. Theorizing that meditation would help my spirits if only I had the appropriate music for it, my Davidson roommate sent a tape with thirty college and university fight songs. With the help

of our expanding team, Joan and I felt we were solving problems as they came up.

❦

*One of the first problems Joan had to face was helping Joe, the self-
reliant can-do husband who almost never asked anyone for help. Watching his strength wane and his body wither, Joan struggled with her changing role in their relationship.*

*"I think my goal, before the diagnosis, was to be like my parents,"
Joan told me, knitting the fingers of her hands around one knee and
leaning back into the afternoon sun that rang through the windows of
their downstairs den. "My parents had sixty-five years of marriage, were
still having a nice life, traveling and enjoying the grandchildren. I thought
that was a nice thing to aspire to, for both of us. Joe and I were just kind
of easily going through a nice life. I felt like we had all the time in the
world, so we didn't have to make goal-plans."*

*All that changed when she made the furtive gesture to the retreating
doctor. Joan had to aggressively help her husband.*

*It's an old idea. Daniel Defoe wrote it down in 1722, paraphrasing
Genesis: "A woman is to be a helpmate and a man is to be the same."
For all the narrowing nametags we give each other nowadays—bread-
winners, homemakers, caregivers, working mothers, self-starters, white-col-
lar mate-seekers, two-career couples, single parents—it's helpmates we
need and helpmates we need to be. And when the conditions of our
mate change, so must the nature of our help. Sitting in her sunny den,
Joan radiated efficient Nordic beauty, smiling broadly and flashing steel-
blue eyes, remembering how foolish she felt when she realized it all came*

down to simply being the woman Joe needed, being herself, letting Joe be Joe.

It happened when she learned that Frank Mayes, the pastoral counselor at their church, wanted Joe to come to the weekly congregational dinner and tell a roomful of people about his experience with ALS. Horrified at the prospect, she declined the invitation for him, "trying to make that evening not happen." She thought, "Poor Joe. He can't talk about this, he'll cry."

It wasn't protection Joe needed, but help in living, one day at a time, one night at a time. What Joe needed from Joan was help in reestablishing his sense of purpose. He very much wanted to talk about life with ALS, and he wanted Joan there with him, not in the audience but at his side. He accepted the invitation Joan turned down and asked her to sit next to him on the stage.

Part of her job that evening—during that first public expression of Joe's new attitude toward living—was to give him a touch now and then, or to whisper a word of caution if she felt he was losing control of his emotions. She was proud of Joe as he spoke, giving help to others who might be in trouble, sharing the advice of Bob Stone and Norman Cousins and Stanley Appel.

Joe told the crowd packed into Covenant's fellowship hall that his job with his illness was to be a conscientious teammate. "Somebody else is doing the research, somebody else is prepared to help me deal with paralysis, somebody else is going to help me if I need some other kind of help. My job in my own recovery is not that complicated: Just get up every morning, go to the ballpark, and do my very best." And that was also a good way for Joan to look at her own sense of purpose: Go to the ballpark, do her best. Only now, the name of Joan's ballpark was Joe.

"It's true," Joe said that night, "that some people can't actually go to the ballpark. Some can't even get up. But people can build their own personal ballpark in which they play out their lives. If they build that ballpark out of love, hope, faith, joy, laughter, festivity, sense of purpose, determination, and will to live, and if they go there every day, they are going to be much better off.

"That's what a community of faith can do," Joe said. "It can help people build environments of love, hope, faith, joy, and all the rest. We can do that for ourselves, for each other—really, for the whole city."

"He's doing just fine," Joan reassured herself. "It's okay. People laugh with him, and they cry with him. It's okay."

Her sense of purpose crystallized. "That moment, I was his side-kick," she recalled. "And actually, I realized then that, this boy, he's doing stuff. He's got a plan here. He's going to talk to people, and I'm going to back him up. Suddenly, Joe and I had a job to do."

Chapter Six

IN THE FIRST WEEK IN 1997, we took all our children and grandson Joseph to Cozumel. Joe B.'s job as a minister prevented his spending Christmas with us, so the family trip was our way of compensating for that. Cozumel is an easy flight from Charlotte, but Joan and I were combining the trip with the January ALS clinic, so we booked our tickets through Houston; we would change planes there on the way down and visit the clinic on the way back.

On the trip from Charlotte to Cozumel, the connection timing in Houston was short and the distance far. For the first time, I agreed to be pushed in a wheelchair. I did not want to do that, but I was relieved not to have to walk so far so fast.

At the resort where we stayed, the distance from the beach to the dining room was great enough that I agreed again to be pushed in a chair. Otherwise, Joan and I would have spent half of each day in transit from beach to food. We had a wonderful week all together, after which I arrived at the clinic in Houston looking like a tanned and healthy Moses.

At the clinic, each patient meets with a dozen or more specialists—pulmonary, physical therapy, nutrition, psychology, neurology, speech pathology, and so on. Since I was having so little functional or physical difficulty, some of my checkups were drive-bys. ("Any problems?" "No." "Any questions?" "No." "Well, see you next time.")

At that January clinic, a physical therapist said to me without any warning that I recognized, "You should use a power scooter to get around."

"I don't really need one," I said. "I'm walking all right, and the distances I have to go are not very great."

"Look," she said, "the biggest threat to your health right now is a fall. If you break something, it will make it much more difficult to deal with the effects of ALS. Just use the scooter to get from one place to another, then leave the scooter and sit or stand. It will reduce the opportunities for falling."

I promised her I would think about it.

I could not think of how to make use of a scooter. My life covered too much geography: home, office, church, and meetings and events all over town. Having a scooter would require having a van to transport it from place to place. So I did nothing.

Within a couple of weeks, a good friend of ours died, and his family asked if I would like to use his scooter and van. Sometimes, providence is pushy.

The scooter was easy but still posed problems. It could not

turn around in the elevators at the bank, so I could not reach
the buttons after driving in. It could not pull up to a desk or
table. Worst of all, it was not always available when I needed it at
the office. I would park it outside my office, and Hugh and Chuck
would constantly take it for joyrides. The scooter's throttle was
marked with a turtle for *slow* and a rabbit for *fast*. Chuck issued
a challenge to Hugh and me: Go all the way around the fifty-
seventh floor, including the four corners, at "full rabbit." We
succeeded mainly in terrorizing the secretaries who sat at desks
in those corners.

With the arrival of the van and the difficulty of loading the
scooter by myself, I had to face a fact: I was going to need some
help on a regular basis, especially if I wanted to continue a reasonable schedule at the office. It was taking me too long to get
ready in the mornings, too long to get from one place to another. I needed an extra right hand for note taking, book carrying, and so on.

I wrote a help-wanted ad for a personal assistant, but I was
stymied by the newspaper's classified categories. I could adver-
tise for a nurse or for medical care, or I could put a personal
under "Men Seeking Men," though the messages there seemed
to be seeking something other than what I was asking. There
was no category for assistance for a person with disabilities. If
anyone sent such a request to the paper, it was printed under
"Domestic Servants." I doubted that the person I was looking
for would be reading ads for domestics.

I took the problem to Chuck. He reminded me that the
company had a "Work/Family" program designed to assist people

with conflicts between their need to be at work and their need to deal with the demands of personal or family life. I knew that, but it had not occurred to me that the program's help was intended for me. That assumption is a standard trap for people in need. Believing that there is no help makes it much harder to find help. Refusing to ask for help makes finding it nearly impossible.

Meanwhile, Chuck assigned Larry Wilson to help me in the mornings temporarily. Larry is a good example of how close help can be when there appears to be none. He was the security officer posted to our floor and had a desk not twenty feet from my office. He was already a friend. What I didn't know about him was that he had been shot while on duty as a city policeman and had spent many months in rehab. Afterward, he had worked at the hospital, giving people precisely the kind of help I now needed. In addition to helping me get ready and getting me to the office, Larry encouraged me to believe we would find a full-time helper with whom I could be comfortable.

The "whom" we found was Andy Baron, and where we found him was in the plumbing department at Home Depot. Andy was practicing one of his best skills: shopping. An acquaintance of his, also shopping, asked what he was doing with his life. ("Nothing," he replied.) The acquaintance then disclosed that she worked for an agency that was looking for a personal assistant for a bank public relations executive.

Andy had no relevant experience or credentials. But he had everything else. He was twenty-nine, living on his own, wondering what to do with his life. After working for several years managing one of his father's health and beauty aids retail stores, he had left the job, traveled around the world scuba diving in places like Papua New Guinea, and diving into his religious and cultural heritage in Israel. More recently, he had spent a couple of months just hanging out and working out at the "J," the Jewish Community Center. He was ready for something to do—"Something demanding," he said, "something not routine or regular, something with the satisfaction of knowing that you're doing some good in the world."

I wanted to sign him immediately. I told him about my upcoming award from the Urban League and about the speech I wanted to make. He accepted the job. No two people were ever better suited for their roles, Andy as caregiver and life manager and I as the recipient of his care.

I told Andy that if I could make it to the end of 1997 still on the job, I would likely get a bonus. I thought it was fair to promise him a bonus, too, if he could keep me going to the office that long. After pondering that over the weekend, he asked me, "Have you ever seen *Weekend at Bernie's?*"

I had. In the movie, a couple of guys go to the beach for a party at Bernie's house and find Bernie dead. To salvage the party, the guys prop Bernie up, take him for a ride and wave his arms at passersby, even take him water-skiing. The results are predictably and stupidly disastrous, but the ruse works. As long as Bernie appears to be alive, the party goes on.

"Don't worry," Andy said. "When bonus time comes, you are going to be sitting at that desk, one way or another."

After Andy's first major assignment, it was unclear which of us would need propping up by year's end.

The Urban League's awards dinner was on March 6, 1997, just a week after Andy started working. Andy helped me into my tuxedo, but Larry drew the ceremonial duty of assisting me up the steps and into my chair on stage. As I settled into the chair—with a bright spotlight on me, with my image magnified on huge screens to my right and left, with nothing between me and more than a thousand people who were watching me sympathetically and intently—I dropped my weakened right hand into my lap and felt my thumb slide into the open zipper.

Two fortuitous facts saved the day. First, the zipper on my tux was a discreet black with a matte finish, rather than the polished metal of zippers on normal pants, so it did not glitter in the spotlight. Second, there was not much I could do with my right hand anyway, so I left it there over the zipper through the entire speech. It was the most productive work that hand had done in a month.

Other than that, the speech went well. I could hear that I made people laugh, I could see that I made them cry, and I could hope that I made them think. The premise was simple: We are quick to find racism in other people and slow to recognize it in ourselves, as if it is somebody else's fault that we spend so much of our lives in monochrome enclaves.

The idea for Race Day—a program in which participants would eat lunch on Thursdays until October with someone of a different racial or ethnic background—began as comic relief in a speech that had some heavy stuff to deliver. But the idea seemed to hit home as a doable thing. And since Charlotte was the NASCAR capital of the world, anyone who might object to what we were doing would probably think Race Day was just a way to honor champion drivers Richard Petty and Jeff Gordon.

People laughed, but they also started setting up Race Day dates immediately. At the end of the dinner, they lined up to tell me how many dates they had already arranged. Some of them brought along their "trophies" for proof. ("See? He's white. We're having lunch next Thursday." "What's his name?" "I don't know yet. But he's white.")

The plan did not have the same impact on everybody. An African American officer of the bank told me, "I have lunch with white people every day. On Thursdays, I'm gonna find me a brother to have lunch with." Fair enough.

As weeks went by, interesting things happened. Young African Americans discovered they could invite corporate CEOs to lunch on Thursdays, thus making clever and very effective career connections. Like everybody else, the CEOs accepted either because they were genuinely interested or because they did not want to get caught not playing the game. Any number of Race Day lunches turned into job opportunities, new customer relationships, or, more than anything else, new friendships.

It took a depressingly small number of weeks for people to run out of names. In a city of a half-million people, a city that prided itself on racial harmony, prominent blacks and whites did not know enough members of the other race to sustain a series of weekly lunches. I began to get calls from people asking if I could recommend "a good white person" or "a black person with similar interests." Andy suggested that we start a Race Day dating service and make some money. Instead, churches and clubs began organizing events.

The news media made such a big deal of the idea that it was a little embarrassing. There was television coverage of people having lunch. There were favorable editorials and massive news stories. My invitations to lunch multiplied to such a degree that Andy and I scheduled them as double dates or even as group events on every day of the week for the next six weeks. After that, I declared a moratorium. Eventually, I figured, someone would recognize that the principal benefit of the whole program was a bunch of free lunches for Andy and me.

I wrote to ask my friends at the newspaper to tone it down a little. "If you thought my idea of having lunch was so brilliant," I teased them, "just wait 'til you hear what I think about mid-afternoon ice cream." They published the line, whereupon we were swamped with invitations for ice cream in the afternoon. It really was one of the great gimmicks of all time. I thought Andy was pushing our luck when he said in an interview that we also liked banana pudding, but it worked like a charm. We had more banana pudding than we knew what to do with.

Andy was proud of what we were doing to focus the community on the possibilities of race relations, and he was my perfect sidekick for Race Day lunches. He was affable and entertaining, but he was also knowledgeable and sensitive. At one lunch, we were met by a reporter for the newspaper. After general discussion of why we were all there together, the reporter concluded with a very odd exercise prescribed by his editors as proper protocol: he asked each person's racial classification. "You are black?" he inquired of the woman next to me.

"Yes."

"And you are white?" he said to me.

"Yes."

And so it went without a hitch around the table, until he reached Andy.

"You're white," the reporter said to Andy. He had already marked the expected answer in his notebook and was putting it away when Andy spoke.

"Actually," Andy said matter-of-factly, "I am African American." I looked at him incredulously. So did everyone around the table. "My people came from Egypt," he explained. "There's a whole book about it. It's called Exodus."

At the office, people gradually came to accept the fact that Andy would be wherever I was, would see whatever I saw, would hear whatever I heard. I gave him a quick lecture on being an insider, on not speculating in bank stocks, on not repeating to anyone else anything he knew that might have any bearing on the future price of our stock. Hugh McColl made the point more effectively. Talking with me about some current problem, Hugh stopped, looked at Andy, and said, "We're gonna have to have you killed."

My relationship with Andy became as close and as comfortable as any relationship I have ever had with anybody. He was by turns like a son, like a brother, like my father, as need be. He made me smile just by arriving in the morning, made me laugh at the zest with which he attacked his role as my barber, slapping preshave on me and then flapping a towel dramatically and threateningly to dry it off. And he made me confident by his ability to cover any awkwardness of mine and to solve any problem.

I looked forward to each day's serious conversations—to his learning about the bank and about corporate life, to our mutual learning about the compatibility of Jewish and Presbyterian views on theology, and to my learning that I was going to be all right. "Joe," he would say each time I apologized for asking him to do something I could no longer do for myself, "if that's the worst thing we ever have to do, we got no problem."

When time came for the trout-fishing trip to the Poconos, Andy said he would take me. We drove the van, so I could have the power chair and Andy would have room for groceries. "I have heard," he said, "how Christians plan things like this. They don't take anything but alcohol. If I'm going, we're going to have food, really good food."

While the other guys were making breakfast of scrambled eggs and coffee, I sat by the fire with my salami-and-onion omelet. For lunch, instead of our usual sandwiches, we had a kettle of Andy's Incredible Chili. We also had some discussion about whether Andy could be invited back in future years even if I could not come.

I could not fish, but Andy did. Still, thanks to my Ranger-X Storm Series power chair, I could get down some fairly steep hills to the edge of the water. The Tobyhanna is a beautiful stream through gorgeous woods, and I loved being out there. I had no mishaps in the woods. Using a walker in the house, however, I fell backwards and cut a gash in the back of my head. When Andy got to me, I was gushing enough blood to scare anyone. With no muss, no fuss, he held a cloth to my head until the bleeding stopped, then helped me to a bed to rest while he cleaned up Bob's floor. He showed no alarm or stress—until we were home and reporting the incident to Joan. Then he confessed to being scared that I had hurt myself really seriously.

In the Poconos, too, I found that I could not hold myself in a standing position and also hold up a heavy bath towel to dry myself after a shower. And when I dropped the towel on the floor, I could not pick it up. "I'm sorry," I called to Andy, a little embarrassed to be standing there naked and helpless. "I need some help."

"Joe," he said as he picked up the towel and started drying me, "if this is the worst thing we ever have to do, we got no problem." It was becoming a familiar refrain.

By October, my speech was so slurred that I needed constant translation, especially for anyone not used to hearing me. This was sometimes awkward for people until they could figure out whether to look at me or at Andy or Joan or whoever might be translating for me.

During one meeting in a conference room near my office, Andy sat between me and a very prominent person in town whom I hardly knew. As Andy watched me carefully and mouthed the words I was trying to form, I said to the visitor, "Aemwi hih ahbihdu heeyuh"—or something to that effect.

Andy turned to the man and translated: "Joe says he is really happy to see you."

The visitor looked at Andy and said, "Please tell Joe that I am very happy to be here."

No one in the room was fast enough to head off the inevitable. Andy turned to me and slurred, "Ee zahbi dubmee ih."

As the communication problem grew worse, I ordered a voice

synthesizer, a DynaMyte by DynaVox Systems. There are simpler and less expensive aids, but I wanted something portable and sophisticated, simple enough for personal conversations but powerful enough to enable me to continue making speeches. The DynaMyte allowed me to alter its basic programming so that I could select one of eight or nine voice options and then change the sound of that voice to approximate mine. I could also change the voice's pronunciation and inflection to sound more natural to an audience of Southerners. By fall, I was using the DynaMyte exclusively for public speeches and fairly often for conversation.

When it became difficult to use a keyboard, I ordered an Eyegaze computer system from LC Technologies and started practicing with it. Using a camera that bounced an infrared light beam off my eyeball, the Eyegaze measured and instantly responded to the movement of my eyes as I looked at a keyboard on the screen in front of me. By pausing on letters or command buttons for a fraction of a second, I could type, place phone calls, "speak," access the Internet, correspond with people, control lights and heat in my home, and even turn on the gas logs in the fireplace!

Still, problems with mobility and communication made it difficult for me to lead the corporate affairs staff at the bank. My group was doing fine and gave no indication that carrying me was an imposition. But we had a plan for an orderly transition, and I worried that the plan would not be carried out unless I initiated it while I still had the time and the credibility to see it through. With concurrence from Hugh and Chuck, I sent a memo:

Charlotte
October 23, 1997

Corporate Affairs Team

Dear gang:

My physical condition has reached a point that requires some rearrangement of my job. I would have said that I need to give up day-to-day management of corporate affairs, but I knew that no one would be able to hear that and keep a straight face.

Mr. McColl has appointed Lynn Drury as Principal Corporate Affairs Officer, reporting directly to him, effective immediately. This is something that Dick Stilley and I have actually discussed over a long period of time, and we are in full agreement with the decision. This is a wonderful promotion that Lynn has certainly earned, but it is also an affirmation of our group, since everybody knows that it is our collective teamwork that makes any one of us successful!

I am very happy to have been asked to stay on as part of the team. I will be "special counsel" to Mr. McColl—and also to Lynn, and to you, and to anyone else that I can catch in my wheelchair (i.e., anyone who cannot run faster than seven miles per hour).

I know that you will join me in congratulating Lynn— and also in promising to keep on making her look good!

Joe

In December, Andy volunteered to get our Christmas tree. He and his friend Steve Garfinkel, an outstanding young immigration lawyer, had never had the experience of picking out a Christmas tree and didn't know if such an opportunity would ever come along again. Selecting the tree proved to be the easy part. It is likely that Andy and Steve were the only Jews in the Christmas tree lot at First Presbyterian, but they examined trees and selected one so suavely that they could easily have been Presbyterians themselves. Then, as all the real Presbyterians were tying down trees atop their cars, Andy and Steve blew their cover by stuffing their tree *inside* the car for the trip home—undoubtedly the first time this had been attempted in all of Christendom. Still, it was as beautiful a tree as we have ever enjoyed.

I had begun the year more or less independent. I had given up driving, given up walking, given up talking. I needed assistance with eating and bathing and brushing my teeth and getting into bed and out of it, needed assistance with essentially everything physical I had to do. And I felt terrific. Through love and through laughter, we had kept the demon of despair at bay. Love and laughter so filled my life that I hardly felt any losses.

I told a Sunday-school class that I had seen a church sign somewhere around town assuring the world that "two can do anything, if one of them is God." In my own experience, I had found that "three can do anything, if one them is God and one of them is Andy." I meant it as a compliment to Andy, who was sitting right beside me, but it also seemed to me to be pretty good theology. Andy and I had in fact formed a little community of faith, doing for each other what a community of faith is supposed to do—leaving human fingerprints on the reality of God's possibilities for our lives.

We both got year-end bonuses.

Joan Martin is the banker of Joe's memory. She tends scrapbooks and photo albums by the dozen. She hoards boxes of newspaper and magazine articles. Letters to Joe exceed the limits of expandable files and overflow into teetering piles. They come by airmail and e-mail, on elegant stationery and ragged-edged sheets ripped from spiral-bound steno pads. "Why don't you take some of these and look through them?" Joan suggested, perhaps in order to clear some space on her dining-room table.

Wandering among all the words, I was struck by the repeated references to Joe's sense of humor, his ability to make people laugh. In fact, there was an entire article from the front page of the Charlotte Observer, *dated January 2, 1998, dedicated to this curious ability. Reporter Bob Meadows's piece was headlined,*

Armed with the Power of Laughter: Joe Martin's humor puts people at ease, opens them to his message

You don't pity Joe Martin. You laugh with him. Sometimes you snicker because what he said wasn't that funny. Other times, you laugh so hard that you double over, hand on stomach, tears rolling down your face, knowing some imaginary drummer just hit ba-dum-bump.

His sense of humor astounds you. Why? Because he uses a

wheelchair. Because he can't speak clearly. Because he has Lou Gehrig's disease. Because of the racism and intolerance he confronted in the past year. . . .

"It's the same as always," he said of his sense of humor. "But my medical condition makes me have a little different effect. Everything seems softer. At the race summit, I said some things that would've aggravated people if I said them four or five years ago. I think because of my situation, people were more receptive, more responsive."

. . . People say Martin is an inspiration. Just being up on stage at the race conference was an inspiration. Coming into the office every day, that's inspiring. Laughing at his disease, making others feel so comfortable, that's inspiring.

"That has puzzled me. I don't feel inspiring," Martin said. "I'm proud how easily I can make people laugh hard, and I think that I've done that. To make them laugh and to make them think, that's deliberate. But the inspiration is something people draw out of themselves when [they] see me."

Then comes that smile again.

"Teddy Roosevelt thought the presidency was a bully pulpit," Martin said. "A wheelchair gets the same advantage. Not only that, but to catch me, [critics] have to be able to run more than seven miles an hour."

Ba-dum-bump.

Shoveling through the mounds of mail, I came across a letter Joe wrote to his teammates at the bank in the spring of 1998 to let them know that, while he found it "very flattering" to be tendered so much favorable publicity, he was in fact "being given way more credit than I deserve." Joe wanted his teammates to know that each of them deserved at least as much praise as he was getting. Referring to an article that found his "fingerprints" on many good things that had happened in the community, Joe wrote his associates, "Those are not my fingerprints; they're ours. Sometimes they're really just yours. . . . Each one of us looks better because all of us are so good together."

Just behind that letter in the box was a response from one of his associates, Walter Elcock. "Fingerprints, my ass," Elcock wrote, daring Joe to deny "the smoking gun" in his own hand. It was Joe's determination, Elcock insisted, that made the difference "between doing good and just being there." Elcock's note concluded with the observation that "the moments of truth are cold and lonely. Thank you for standing watch on so many cold nights. Thank you for your silence in the clamor and your presence in the void."

Another letter was from a corporate teammate Joe had never met, Brian Fogle, who suddenly found himself working for NationsBank when it bought the Midwest's largest bank, Boatmen's. After viewing a tape of Joe's Urban League remarks, Fogle wrote, "The fact that our organization greatly values such a man as you and recognizes those contributions you have made speaks volumes to me about the kind of company that we are. We are so fortunate to have you in our organization and especially such an integral part of it. We are more fortunate to realize what you bring to us in compassion, creativity and commitment. . . . I suspect there are countless others who feel the same way I do. The pebbles you have tossed in the pond in Charlotte have sent ripples reaching Missouri. I just felt the need to let you know that."

In another box was a letter written in the summer of 1997, when one of Joe's ripples hit the Canadian Rockies. A young woman who was a friend of the Martin family, Joanie Fleming, had been hiking the mountains with a buddy. After a grueling day, Joanie found herself thinking about Joe and told her friend about him. "That instantaneously lifted our spirits," she wrote to Joan Martin. "I wonder if Mr. Martin knows how many spirits he lifts?"

Another lifted spirit was that of Dr. John Chiles, who heard Joe speak at their alma mater, Davidson College, in the fall of 1997. On that occasion, Joe was honored with the school's first John W. Kuykendall Award for community service. In his address that day, Joe said that Davidson students had been taught to combine the life of the mind with a life of faith, but that they needed also to "cultivate the life of the heart." Dr. Chiles wrote the college's alumni magazine of his intention to follow that advice. He quoted William Butler Yeats's grim simile of the passing years as "great black oxen" goaded on by God, with men "broken by their feet." Dr. Chiles observed that while "most of us know what is right, and know a hundred little important reasons not to do it just now, . . . for Joe, thinking and doing the right thing have become the same. He is living by his heart. There is no black ox stepping on Joe."

Sometimes, Joe's ripples come back in curious patterns. Reading through the reams of correspondence between Joe and the world, I came across a quote from Dr. Martin Luther King. It was in a letter from a young writer named Issac Bailey, who was hoping Joe would help him get a few job interviews. It seemed that Bailey believed Joe might feel somehow connected to a black man who had attended Davidson, which had not admitted its first black student until the year after Joe graduated. Everything in life is interrelated, wrote Issac Bailey, quoting Dr. King. Every one of us is part of an ineludible network, so that whatever affects one affects all. None of us can achieve his potential until all of us become what we ought to be. We are tied "in a single garment of destiny."

Indeed, all the letters and articles in all Joan's boxes and folders and piles spoke to this same point. Wrapped tighter than most of us in that garment of destiny, Joe greets each day determined to be the man he ought to be on that day. By so doing, he helps each one of us become the man or woman we ought to be. On any given day, Joe believes that this is the day the Lord has made, for all of us and for each of us.

Joe and Joan at home, summer 1995

Joe with Hugh McColl at a Carolina Panthers game,
November 1996
PHOTOGRAPH BY JAN BROWN

*Joe and Joan with Larry and Katherine Youngblood in the
British Virgin Islands, February 1995*

At the lake, June 1999
*From left: Neil Cottrell, Larry Youngblood, Joe, Susan Abbott, Dottie
Martin, Jim Martin, Joan's sister Katherine Youngblood, Tony Abbott*
PHOTOGRAPH BY JOAN MARTIN

Jodi, Joe B., Joe, David, Elizabeth; December 1994
PHOTOGRAPH BY JOAN MARTIN

*Joe B. with Joseph, Benjamin with Jodi, Elizabeth, David with
his black Lab, Joan, and Joe; Thanksgiving 1999*

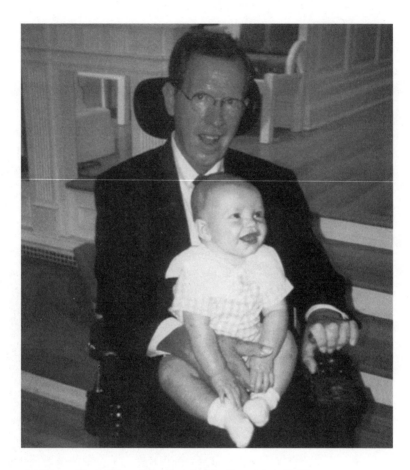

Giving Benjamin a ride after church, September 1998

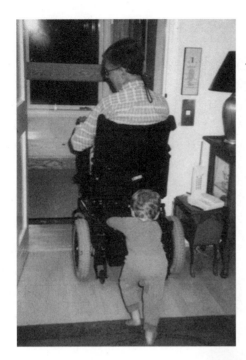

Joseph pushes PopPop's power chair into the elevator, April 1998
PHOTOGRAPH BY JOAN MARTIN

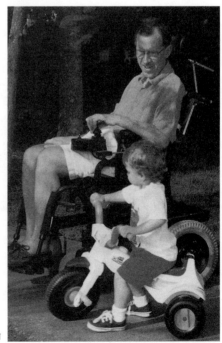

Racing with Joseph, June 1998
PHOTOGRAPH BY JOAN MARTIN

Joe cycling with Andy Baron, April 1997
PHOTOGRAPH BY JOAN MARTIN

Daris Elliott, May 1999
PHOTOGRAPH BY JOAN MARTIN

Off on a fishing trip with Andy, May 1997
PHOTOGRAPH BY JOAN MARTIN

On stage before a speech with Jamie, Neil, and Rusty, November 1998
PHOTOGRAPH BY JOAN MARTIN

Joe with Chuck Cooley and Nancy Dry at a wedding, April 1999

Joe in Norway with Jamie and Rusty, August 1999
PHOTOGRAPH BY NEIL COTTRELL

Joe and Joan, August 1997

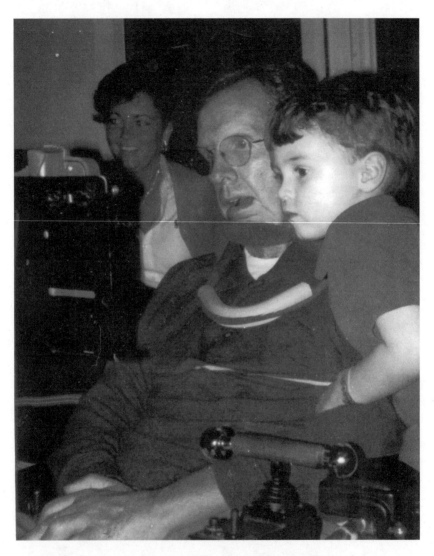

Playing with Joseph by voice synthesizer, with Joan's assistant
Katie Boyer in the background, February 2000
PHOTOGRAPH BY JOAN MARTIN

Chapter   Seven

A S WINTER SETTLED IN during late 1997 and the early part of 1998, I wondered whether we would be able to repeat the previous year's family vacation in the Caribbean sunshine. Our travel agent went to work on the problem of accessibility. He recommended the Beaches resort at Negril, located not too far from Montego Bay, Jamaica. There was an easy, direct flight from Charlotte. We would enjoy activities and facilities for adults and children—all fully accessible.

Accessible is a flexible term with regard to bathrooms, even in the United States. At Beaches/Negril, there were a couple of grab bars beside a conventional tub. Andy had to lift me into the tub and hold me up while he showered me. "Joe," he said, "if this is the worst thing we ever have to do, we got no problem." I decided I had a choice: I could let Andy and others help me, even with intimate chores, or be embarrassed and stay home and miss out on the rest of my life. It was an easy choice for me, even easier for Andy. We chose life—and/or Jamaica.

Still, Andy let me know in his own subtle way that he might have limits. He told a story of a guy whose hunting buddy was bitten on his private parts by a snake. The guy left his buddy in the woods and ran into town to ask a doctor what to do. He was told, "Either you have to suck out the poison or your friend is going to die." When he returned to the woods, his buddy asked what the doctor had said. The guy looked at him solemnly and reported, "The doctor said you are going to die."

Whatever problems I developed, I figured they would never be that bad.

In Jamaica, I was the only person at the resort with a wheelchair, yet I never felt that I was different from other guests. With the exception of an upstairs piano bar, all the activities were easy for me to get to. The staff members were friendly and helpful when I needed help. They never acted as if there was anything unusual about me.

There were trails for me to explore in the power chair, often with Joseph in my lap. Once, when we passed a young family, I heard a child say, "Look, Dad, they're giving rides!" Only the sand beach proved a problem for my chair, so we borrowed a lighter push chair to get me to "our" cabana and lounge chairs.

Andy had a great time scuba diving, snorkeling, windsurfing, reading, talking his way behind the bar to take charge of mixing our drinks, becoming pals with the entire staff. He did not neglect me by any means. In fact, he took such good care of me that, for the first time in a long while, Joan felt totally relaxed—

free to do whatever she wanted without worrying about leaving me behind.

When I stayed inside to work on the computer while everyone else sat in the sun, Andy set his watch to sound an alarm every twenty minutes, at which time he would say, "David"—or the next in line—"it's time to go check on your dad." They needed, he explained to me, "some quality time with their father." And Andy needed sun.

Late in the week, they were all in the hot tub by the pool. "Can you believe it?" Andy lamented. "Just two more days and we have to go back to work."

"Andy," Elizabeth reminded him, "you *are* working!"

"Oh, yeah."

A couple of months later, our grandson Joseph crossed over into the terrible territory that follows a second birthday. Things changed. The first year of his life, he had sat in my lap and ridden along with me. Before he could talk, he would lean back against me and mimic the humming sound of a car. When I picked up speed, or if he wanted to go faster, he would lean into me harder and hum louder. Then, as he began to walk and talk, he would sometimes push me, flattening his body out behind me as if all four hundred pounds of power chair and grandfather depended entirely on him. Or he would ride and give directions: "This way, PopPop. No, that way."

At two, he stopped riding in my lap. Been there, done that. He preferred—insisted on—riding his own tricycle. And he took charge of our relationship. He loved speeding down the sloping, curving sidewalk at the lake and would do that all alone, over and over. But whenever I was outside, he would call, "Come on, PopPop!" and we would race down together. Then he would go back to the top of the hill and call me to come. When I had enough and preferred to sit and watch him, he would wait at the top of the hill, absolutely silent and absolutely still, until I joined him for another ride.

I was afraid of losing my relationship with Joseph through my increasing inability to play. That fear turned to fascination at his efforts to figure out what to do with me. At our house, he would go into the elevator, close the metal accordion door, and call, "Come on, PopPop!" When I would drive my chair into the door, rattling the whole elevator, he would laugh so hard he fell down on the floor. Over and over. One day, after he apparently noticed that I could not speak clearly, he led me around the house pointing to objects and saying their names. "Table, PopPop." "Chair." "Apple."

At Christmastime, three months shy of Joseph's third birthday, we were at his house, where there wasn't sufficient room inside to ride his trike or my chair. He tried several approaches, without success.

"Come on, PopPop," he said, standing on the steps to his room.

"PopPop's chair can't go upstairs," said Elizabeth, his "Aunt Z."

"Oh, sorry," he said.

Then he walked around the room, apparently deep in thought. He put his prize toy, Thomas the Tank Engine, in my lap. No results, since I could not reach for the toy or hold it or push it.

Finally, Joseph put his hands on my knees and grinned up at

me. I moved one knee ever so slightly—which was about as far as I was able to move it. Bump. He shrieked in mock surprise and ran away laughing. Then he came back to my knees, waiting with his little grin. Bump, shriek, flight, laughter, and back to my knees, over and over and over.

Joseph had taught me the happiness of minimalist festivity. His requirements of me were simple. I had to be present. I had to be patiently available to him. And I had to allow him to create little moments of festivity for both of us. The incipient depression of becoming a spooky and useless grandfather gave way to an eagerness for Joseph's little brother, Benjamin, to have his turn. And in time, perhaps, for little cousins to have theirs.

ALS does not affect a number of things, they say—eyesight, for example, and bowels. The doctors are unanimous and adamant about this. But the doctors do not have ALS. Ask any of us who have the disease. We are also unanimous and adamant: there is a problem with bowels. Ask Andy.

Rather unexpectedly, given that I had read all the medical literature on this subject, constipation began to require a greater and greater share of my daily sense of purpose. At one point, Andy and I figured we were spending half of every day working on human rights and the other half working on a bowel movement. On most days, it was difficult to say which was more challenging, or more rewarding.

Drugstore remedies were ineffective, and doctors were uninterested. So we were on our own, up that creek without a paddle. This was not humorous. I was miserable. Eventually, I had to spend two full days every week in painful hard labor for one bowel movement. During that time, I honestly did not care whether I lived or not.

On one particularly miserable afternoon, Andy phoned for advice from Dr. Bill Bullock, the physician who has tended to our family for twenty-five years and who had spotted the possibility of ALS in my very first symptom. When I heard Andy ask Joan if we had rubber gloves, I knew that the good doctor was telling him how to break up impacted bowels. But not to worry. Andy hung up the phone, looked at me solemnly, and reported, "Well, the doctor said you are going to die." In spite of myself, I laughed.

I mention this unseemly subject as a reminder that, while life goes on in the face of a traumatic diagnosis or event, the difficulties of the situation do not just go away. I acknowledge that the pains and stresses and fears that some people endure are more difficult and more persistent than mine. But whatever the problems are, to the extent that people keep them alive and in mind, they must deal with those problems, over and over if necessary, as a precondition to finding any higher sense of purpose. People not in trauma will not understand, but constipation or an ingrown toenail or a messy garage can take on life-or-death significance without help from somewhere.

The solution to my difficulty was far more simple than the trail-breaking problem of getting anyone to take it seriously. After a month or so of pure misery, I managed to harass all my doctors so persistently that one of their eminences finally gave me the answer: four uncooked prunes every night. Ultimately, we discovered that they could be blended into a milkshake from Ben & Jerry's with the same effect. Life is good.

My mother, of course, could have answered the question a lot faster than the doctors, had I thought to ask her. She was a source of strength to me all through the ordeal of coping with the diagnosis. Atypically—at least for the first time in my life, if not in hers—she delivered that strength by example, rather than by instruction. In the past, I had said in her presence and to her apparent delight that my father was put on this earth to be an example to his sons, while my mother was put here to make sure we didn't miss the point. She set standards. And she kept score.

I worried about the effect on her of having to watch her son struggle with a paralyzing condition when no one could offer her any hope of his survival. I worried that she might feel she was losing some support she had counted on for her old age. At the time of my diagnosis, she was eighty-two. None of us thought of her as having reached old age yet.

She did not show me that my condition was anything more than seriously interesting to her. She did not pry into my prospects, but rather treated the disease in very practical terms. She did ask a couple of times if anything hurt ("No, ma'am"), and she asked me to show her how I got in and out of my chair and the car and how I put on a coat. Generally, she had some technique or some piece of equipment she had mastered that she thought I should try. She seemed pleased at how well we were coping.

She never showed me the grief that I surely caused her, never showed me any reluctance to be with me or any impulse to be with me more than usual—and never showed me any mercy in dominoes. My diagnosis did not seem to compromise either her independence or mine or to change our relationship.

When Pop died in 1982, Mama had declined to move to Charlotte to be near Jim and Dottie and Joan and me. ("I'll just stay in Columbia, where I'm 'Mary Martin' and not 'somebody's mother.'") She moved into a retirement center, where she had quite a few longtime friends from all around the state. She was independent—sufficiently independent to be able to lock the door of her apartment and drive off to Charlotte or to join us at the lake and be "somebody's mother" whenever she chose to.

At the lake was where she was when she died at eighty-five. Her death was, even at that age, sudden and totally unexpected. She had spent the weekend with three of her sons and most of our children and grandchildren. On Monday morning, after checking the plants in Dottie's garden, she felt ill and asked Dottie and Joan to take her to the doctor. She was seriously and obviously ill, but when Joan opened the door to the back seat of the car for her, she said, "I always sit in the front," and walked around the car to the front passenger seat. On the way to the clinic, she gave instructions of what the doctor should be told to check. She then slumped forward, and Joan and Dottie could see that she was not going to make it. They held on to her.

They arrived at the clinic in less than ten minutes. By the time a nurse brought a wheelchair to the car, Mama had already opened her own door. "Are you Mrs. Martin?" the nurse asked.

"Yes, I am," Mama said. "And who might you be?" The next

question would certainly have been, "And where do you go to church?" But she never got to ask it.

My mother was fully alive until the moment of her death. She had struggled with arthritis most of her adult life; she acknowledged it as a burden but never used it as an excuse. She married into a family—and produced one of her own—in which she was surrounded by people with college educations and advanced degrees. She often claimed her high-school diploma as a disadvantage but never as a handicap—more like a battle flag.

She took her roles seriously: being a wife to her husband, an effective partner in his career, and a mother to her sons, to their wives, to their children, and, if need be, to their friends. In fulfilling those responsibilities, she found it useful, if not unavoidable, to be a force in the wider world around her. When the roles of wife and mother were taken away from what we thought was the center of her life, she went right on with undiminished power and purpose.

Her funeral sermon was preached by a man who had been her minister for ten years, a man who never even knew her husband or her children. As we laughed at his respectful but vivid description of her force in the church, in the community, and certainly in the preacher's own life, it became clear that the Mary Martin he knew in her last years was precisely the one we had known since her young adulthood.

I sat in my wheelchair at the funeral, moping a bit about the strength only I (and she!) knew I had lost with her death. But it was hard to miss the last point—the constant point—she had made. The business of being who you are, fully and faithfully, and of doing what you are given to do, despite all the temptations and all the excuses to do otherwise, provides meaningful purpose for our lives. Without this, no other sense of purpose can ring true.

I don't know what greater strength she could have given me.

But my physical strength continued to deteriorate. Changes in the multiple muscles involved in swallowing brought on the choking that terrifies every ALS patient—and everyone who is nearby when it happens. I assumed that the progressive nature of ALS meant that every symptom and every dysfunction or disability would get worse. If I choked on something, I would never eat it again. I was gradually reducing my diet to pureed foods, and I was giving up the social life that revolved around meals. I was losing weight and friends. I never considered the possibility that things might get better.

Neil Cottrell materialized at exactly the right time to help. He was a friend of a friend of Andy's. There is a theory that everyone in the world is connected to everyone else by no more than six degrees of separation—every single person is known to someone who is known to someone, and so on through six of these relationships until you reach someone known to that first person. With Andy, the world was even simpler; everybody in it was a friend of at least one of his friends. Two degrees of separation were as far as Andy ever had to go.

So when the requirements for taking care of me threatened to monopolize Andy's life as well as Joan's, he found Neil, who started out part-time and fairly quickly became a full-time addition to our staff. Neil had graduated from college with a degree in biology and a strong concentration in athletic training. He was interested in physical therapy and occupational therapy and had been working for a year at a rehab center, where he gained experience with patients in need of long-term care. My choking episodes and my many needs were not strange to him.

The awful, involuntary noises I made when I choked scared the living daylights out of me and anybody within earshot, including everybody in the restaurant or in the whole neighborhood. When Neil was with me, I noticed that he remained calm—too calm, I thought. He seemed poised, maybe, but he did not react very fast. "The noise means you are breathing," he explained. "If you stop making noise, I'll help you."

Neil's calm caused me to pay less attention to the noise and panic and more attention to the breathing. I found that I would expel air involuntarily and violently until I had none left, then I would just as involuntarily and just as violently gulp air and start the process over again. Though I was frightened, I imagined that in the worst case I would pass out—and then I would breathe. This was not a terribly comforting thought, but it was better than the expectation of choking to death. I began to concentrate more on the possibility of breathing and less on the possibility of dying.

I found that breathing in was easier, though just as noisy, if I tilted my head forward. Since part of the panic impulse was to throw my head back, I had Neil and Joan and Andy all primed to help hold my head slightly forward. I continued to choke fairly regularly, but I was able to reduce the amount of time it took to get the choking under control.

The panic did not go away entirely. One night when Joan and I were alone at the lake, I choked long after supper, while I was getting ready for bed. It was the worst episode ever, and I thought I was very close to testing my theory about passing out. In that moment of panic, I was not at all confident that I had been right in thinking that I would then resume breathing. I panicked even more, realizing that we could not get to an emergency room very fast, that Joan could not even get me to the car, that we had no simple or quick way of telling a 911 officer how to reach our house.

Next day, I asked Andy to find out where the rescue squad was and to post the directions from their location to ours beside every telephone in the house. But that turned out to be the last time I really choked.

It is certainly true that between breathing and swallowing, breathing is far more critical. Neil showed me that if I concentrated on relaxing and reestablishing a normal flow of air, instead of panicking and trying to clear the food from my throat, I could generally avoid the stress—and the appearance—of choking. And I could then calmly swallow or cough up whatever it was that was causing me a problem. First priority: Calm down and breathe. Replacing fear and stress with confident management reduced the likelihood of choking in the first place.

Moreover, I found with the help of the clinic staff that if I held my head at a certain angle when eating, if I ate slowly and stayed calm, and if I deliberately "thought" each bite through the entire process of chewing and swallowing, I could eat a lot of things that I had given up. Neil was terrific at keeping meals steady, calm, and stress-free even when we went out, and I recovered a reasonably normal diet.

I also had trouble drinking, particularly thin liquids like water. I began to use a straw even with milkshakes, mainly because I couldn't hold the glass up but also because it was hard to manage a big mouthful of anything. When I lost the power to close my lips tightly around a straw and could not suck anything far enough through a straw to get it to my mouth, I thought I would have to quit drinking anything and somehow find another way to get fluids.

The nutritionist on the Houston clinic staff was anything but an ideologue. She took a very practical view of getting enough nourishment, whatever the problem. She was assisted by a cookbook of wonderful recipes compiled by Vicki Appel, the nurse (and Stan Appel's wife) who started the Houston clinic and for whom it was named after her death in 1997. The nutritionist also knew products and techniques that encouraged people to eat. And she could improvise. When I told her that I was worried about getting enough fluids because it was difficult to swallow thin liquids, she asked, "Have you tried frozen daiquiris?" The rest of that summer was great. Dehydration was not a problem.

Andy decided it was time to try water again. He filled a cup with lukewarm water. I tilted my head down and swallowed. It was much easier than managing the stream of water coming through a straw. I swallowed again. No problem.

"You can't imagine," I said to Andy, "how good it feels to gulp like that." It had been maybe a year since I last swallowed a gulp of water. Now, I could do it at will.

It was another lesson for me: Do not assume that when some function becomes difficult or impossible that it will go away forever. There may be a way to coax it back—or a different way to do it.

By the summer of 1998, the time had come for Andy to get on with his life. He had fallen in love with a wonderful young woman in the D.C. area, and he was anxious to move closer to her. He interviewed with our bank there and was accepted for the consumer banking training program.

His impending departure proved that depression can be a recurring problem. I grieved at the prospect of what would happen to my life. I needed more and more help, and my main man was about to vanish. I imagined that I would need the care of a nursing home, imagined that I would become bedridden, imagined that we would begin to shut life down. Andy had become so much a part of my life—actually part of my identity—that I could not imagine carrying on without him.

In retrospect, it seems that my reaction called into question whether an ALS patient can make rational decisions about life support or anything else while in depression. There were days when I did not want to get out of bed. There were days when I refused to get up, easily convincing everybody that I was "just tired." There were days when I stayed under the covers all day long. There were enough such days to prove the point: My days were better when I broke the gloom or when someone intervened and broke it for me. I don't know how many different ways that could have been accomplished in my case at that time, but the way it was done was by solving the problem.

Neil began to fill in for Andy more and more, and my confidence in him grew rapidly. He insisted on stretching me regularly, and that made me feel better immediately. It undoubtedly improved circulation in my legs and arms, but it also gave me a feeling of achievement—and it was something I had to get up for.

Neil signed up two of his friends, Jamie Kuykendall and Rusty McDonald, for part-time work. I was impressed with both of them.

Jamie, almost thirty years old, had worked with Neil at the rehab center and was confident and comfortable with everything I needed. He had decided to go to graduate school in occupational therapy but could commit to us until then. He was conscientiously professional but could break through the most dismal of mornings with a wisecrack that I could not ignore. "I know you're a banker," he said as he was brushing my teeth for the first time. "I was expecting two rows of teeth." Once I laughed, it was very hard to go back to being dismal. Lord knows, I tried. Dismal was comfortable. But Jamie wouldn't go there, and eventually I had to give it up. Over time, I learned that my smile first thing in the morning was as important to him as his was to me.

Jamie's range of interests brought surprising benefits. He loved working in the garden, repairing things around the house, figuring out new assistive equipment, and making things in his woodworking shop. An experienced traveler, he made it easy to believe I could continue taking trips with his help. I felt he made me more complete because, through him, I could get things done that I would have done myself but for my paralysis.

Rusty was Neil's college roommate. Like Neil, he was a biology major with coursework in athletic training. They had grown up in small towns near Charlotte and had become friends when they were teenagers. At twenty-four and twenty-three, they looked like they had been sent from central casting for roles as squadron leaders. Tall, broad-shouldered, athletic, and smart, they were at ease with any assignment. My work at the bank, our travel schedule, and our life in general threw Neil and Rusty into unfamiliar circumstances fairly often, and their delight in new experiences revived my expectation that I could continue doing interesting things.

Neil and Jamie and Rusty convinced us and convinced Andy that Joan and I would be in good hands after he left. The three of them turned out to be remarkable—always positive, always confident, always encouraging, always patient, and always incredibly attentive. They restored our confidence and our spirits.

In many ways, my life must seem like a storybook: *Little Lord Fauntleroy Copes with Trouble*, perhaps. Here I am bopping off to Houston—or, more preposterously, to the Caribbean—hiring staff left and right, ordering expensive computer equipment for home and office, installing brick ramps and elevators with windows, even getting a taller toilet for the private black-marble bathroom attached to my office on the fifty-seventh floor (which is, by the way, the best seat in the house, offering an unobstructed view of the Blue Ridge Mountains more than a hundred miles away).

Few people have the resources I enjoy. Just the same, I know people who are managing ALS effectively with very limited funds.

They are the real heroes in our group. For starters, they know that money is not the only resource, not even the most important one. Friends and family are far more important. Creativity and perseverance are more important. And one's determination to "find a way" is essential; without it, all the money in the world won't help.

Most of the resources I have can be replicated by a group of friends, a civic club, a congregation, a neighborhood, a church circle, a bridge club, a team. What's required is that someone take the initiative—if not the person with ALS or some other trauma, then someone close to that person. The chemistry for coping is all around us, but someone has to turn on the Bunsen burner. (I probably should try some metaphor more familiar to me; Jim will flinch when he reads that one.)

On any given day, any given person can do something toward creating a healing environment. The elements in that environment are really rather simple. Love. Hope. Faith. Joy. Laughter. Festivity. Sense of purpose. Determination. Will to live.

Sure, each of these elements has a complicated form, but a little creativity can help identify manageable aspects. *Faith*, as an easy example, can be an intimidating thing to discuss with someone who's in deep trouble, but it's simple to offer a prayer for someone or to ask for one. Some days, a *sense of purpose* in life may be hard to come by, but a need to try a recipe or to identify the people in an old family photograph or to cast a vote in a church committee or to be a fourth for bridge might be enough to get a person through the afternoon. And *determination* may be a simple matter of reciting the list every day and finding one thing to do in one area. Love. Hope. Faith. Joy. Laughter.

Festivity. Sense of purpose. Determination. Will to live.

This is not to overlook complicated things like medical care and assistive technology. Professional help is essential—and often very hard to find. Locating the right care, checking on insurance coverage, arranging logistics for getting to the right place, and learning about assistive equipment are examples of help that friends can give. Becoming the patient's advocate with the insurance company will remove a huge amount of stress from the patient and the family.

Many of the things that are essential for recovery or for living are incredibly expensive. But those things that are beyond the reach of most individuals are easily within the grasp of a caring community. Clinics and helping agencies and religious congregations can be made inviting, can be made known to people who need them, and can be alerted to what is needed.

What is needed first is to break through the isolation of the trauma. Sometimes, the only resource required is desire. And there's no way around it: each of us bears the primary and very personal responsibility for tapping into that inner resource.

Daris Elliott was a cute little boy who followed Joan home from school. She was tutoring fifth- and sixth-graders as part of a mission project of our church, and Daris was in her class. When she had the children write to colleges to ask for information, Daris chose UNLV, then the reigning NCAA basketball champion. They sent him a brochure about their summer basketball camp, along with a cover letter thanking him for his interest.

"They want me," he reported to Joan. This was not a misunderstanding on his part. It was a way of looking at the world. A kid with no resources of his own, Daris was somehow convinced that the world expected him to succeed and that the world would help him if he asked.

During the year that Joan tutored Daris, his grandfather, with whom he had been living, died. Daris seemed to cling a little closer to Joan, and I began to understand what a remarkable kid he was.

He was moved constantly, shuttled among relatives who let him stay but often did not take much responsibility for him. His mother, who had borne him while she was in high school, was a beautiful and loving young woman. But she was seriously ill and had meager resources to share.

Daris persevered. With nothing more than a will to succeed, he pieced together a support system of his grandmothers, teachers, friends, and more than a few total strangers who received a phone call from Daris because he had heard they could coach a team or drive a van or find a job for somebody.

He was one of only two young people from his neighborhood to finish high school, and the only one to go to college. And he became a leader. Time and again, as Joan and I have met new friends and classmates of his, often from wealthy and educated families, we have been struck by their dependence on Daris for advice and guidance. And his advice always begins with his own view of the world: no fretting, no looking back, no blaming. Where you are is where you start, and the only question worth asking is, "Now, what's the most we can do with this set of circumstances?"

Reality is where wholeness has to begin, where recovery has to begin, where Daris begins, where all of us begin every day. But Daris begins with a generous and positive view of his reality, and that gives him a basis for moving on, for making something good of a reality that would destroy—has destroyed—other people.

Daris Elliott was one of the speakers at the Urban League dinner the night I first encountered Joe, the night Joe challenged people to sit down together and discuss race, rather than ignore it.

Joe received dozens of letters from people in his native South Carolina thanking him for his Race Day idea. In Columbia's newspaper, The State, columnist Julia Sibley wrote that Joe's Urban League speech "stuck in my head, tumbling around like so much wet laundry—heavy with meaning. What if we took on recognition as a goal and from there pledged to work toward reconciliation? We need to recognize before we can reconcile."

The Urban League and the chamber of commerce in Greenville, South Carolina, asked for a videotape of Joe's speech. They played it before a packed multiracial audience at a gathering they called "One Day," so named to proclaim the event as the promise of Martin Luther King's "I Have a Dream" speech. When Joe's tape was over, a powerfully built African American stepped to the microphone, still wiping his eyes. He said, "You heard a gentleman speaking to you from the depth of his soul—from a lifetime of experiences, from a lifetime of interactions with other human beings—who sees that his days are becoming numbered, and that he will no longer be here. He wishes to share with us something of a legacy, to leave to you and to me a chance to do what individually he cannot, but which, collectively, we have the opportunity to do. That is to look at each other face to face, to talk about our strengths and our weaknesses, to talk about our differences and our alikeness."

The speaker was Merl Code, an attorney and judge in Greenville, a member of the chamber's board, and a former player in the National Football League. Code and other community leaders called on Greenville to walk through the door Joe Martin had opened for them. "We need to meet and know you," the black judge said to the white faces in the audience. "We need to talk to one another. I need to tell you when I am disturbed about something. And you need to share it with me. . . . It starts with one person at a time. You and me."

He was talking about more than solving the problems created by racial differences. Merl Code was talking about the problems of life. There were individual conditions, problems, sicknesses, traumas faced by every man and woman in that room. None of them had chosen to bring those problems on themselves, just as none of them had chosen which race to be born into. "You didn't choose to be white, I didn't choose to be black. That choice was made for each of us, prior to our arrival. But what we do once we get here is up to us. What you and I do—for, with each other—is up to us."

Throughout South Carolina's Upstate region, restaurants began offering coupons and discounts for multiracial lunch groups that flashed the One Day membership card. The sponsors refused to give out statistics of how many people were getting together, insisting that this was not about numbers. They would only say that the lunch discount cards were disappearing by the thousands, as fast as they could print them.

The luncheon to celebrate the first anniversary of the One Day program was scheduled for October 28, 1998, in the Palmetto Expo

Center, a barnlike convention facility in central Greenville. The sponsors invited Joe, but they'd been told that his mobility was severely restricted, and they doubted he would actually attend. The week before the event, Joe e-mailed them that he would indeed be there. Word went out, and all four hundred seats were spoken for within a few days. More people came to hear Joe than attended the event at the other end of the Expo Center, where conservative talk-show host G. Gordon Liddy was holding forth.

In the audience were my wife, Jo Ann, and I, sitting up front with Joe, Joan, and Neil Cottrell, who by that time had taken over from Andy as Joe's number one. It was the first time we had attended a function like this with them, and only the second time Jo Ann had seen Joe since the Urban League gathering eighteen months earlier. No sooner was lunch served than a large screen at the front of the hall lit up with a tape of Joe's Urban League address. Occasionally clinking their forks on the institutional china but otherwise silent, the crowd took in Joe's every word. In the semidarkness, Neil folded a washcloth and put it in Joe's mouth.

Joe-on-the-screen didn't need a washcloth. He didn't drool. Joe-on-the-screen could still speak. Joe-at-the-table, overwhelmed by emotion when he heard his big-screen image say, "Racism is a terrible kind of diagnosis," let out a little whimper. Joan put her hand on his knee and gave it a squeeze. Joe-on-the-screen recited his "lovehopefaith" mantra. A TV news cameraman turned on his rude light to capture on videotape Joe-at-the-table watching Joe-on-the-screen. Surreally enough, Joe-watching-Joe would make the evening news.

When Joe-on-the-screen made his joke about how people would

think Race Day was about Richard Petty and Jeff Gordon, the live Joe—always his own best audience—let out a hearty laugh. The wash-cloth fell from his mouth; Neil knelt beside Joe's chair, tenderly blotting the saliva from his chin. As the videotape neared its conclusion, someone signaled Joe to go up to the stage. As the lights came up, he and Neil were still maneuvering up a long ramp. Everyone in the enormous hall stood and applauded, as though it were a noble thing he was doing, just being there, charging on to the stage. They were cheering Joe for living.

After the applause ran its course, there were awkward minutes of silence as Neil worked with a house electrician to plug Joe's voice box into the public-address system. This had been rehearsed in advance, but something wasn't right. Finally, Joe clicked his pointer in the appropriate screen-box, and his electronic voice said, "Excuse me." There was an-other pause, followed by, "Thank you very much."

The impact on the audience was astounding. They had been atten-tive to Joe's Urban League speech and more than receptive to its mes-sage. But the silence that wrapped the hall now was something ap-proaching reverence. I wondered if Joe felt it. Suddenly, before had been replaced by after. There for all to see was the terrible black magic of Lou Gehrig's disease. Joe of the quick repartee, of the firm, expressive voice, of the audience interplay—Joe of the videotaped past—had metamorphosed into this awkward, almost motionless, voiceless Joe of the present. They saw instantly what ALS had done—and they saw just as instantly what it had not done. It had not stopped him from living each moment and filling each moment with his deep sense of purpose.

As usual, Joe started with a couple of laughs. His synthesizer tried out its Southern drawl. Then he thanked the chairman, Baxter Wynn, for inviting him. Wynn was a white Baptist minister and probably fig-ured, Joe said, that having lunch with a Presbyterian would count as "diversity" in Baptist South Carolina. Joe knew his audience; they roared. Then he asked them to consider why it was important for people to get to know those different from themselves.

"We have been walking around for a hundred years or more carry-ing a heavy load, a heavy load of racial suspicion, anger, guilt—and, always, frustration. Walking around watching each other across the rail-road tracks, across racial railroad tracks and fences that we have inherited or that we've built ourselves. Watching each other, wondering what's in that heavy load the other person is carrying."

Again, I was struck by the fact that Joe's description of race-centered anguish could be applied to almost any kind of pain. How much did any of us really understand the nature of our neighbor's burden? Even if we seemed to have a hundred things in common, we could not help one another unless we confirmed the deeper truths of who we were and where we hurt.

"Breaking bread together, reaching across the table to find just one new friend, will hasten the day when we can lay that burden down," Joe assured his audience. "One day, surely one day, we will look at each other and say, 'No more,' and just let that heavy burden go." Joe told them to appreciate the strength of the community's diversity and to "har-ness the power. But don't get carried away dreaming of that day. On this day, today, ask yourself what you can do with just one day."

The standing ovation that followed Joe's speech suggested that the crowd had caught the underlying sense of daily practical purpose. He was not dreaming of some future "one day" in the next life or cowering in fear of "one day" when this life would end. He was using this one day, today, to fulfill his purpose. For Joe, this was the day that had been given and was the day to be used. On any given day, any miracle might be possible.

Afterward, people crowded around our table to hug Joe or pat him on the shoulder. The next day's Greenville News—*in an article headlined "Greenville Visit Shows Illness Hasn't Stopped Crusader for Racial Unity"—included several of those reactions.*

Heather Gatchell of the chamber said, "I was not prepared for Joe Martin."

B. J. Koonce agreed: "He was so dynamic."

Merl Code, now president-elect of the chamber, told Joe, "You have inspired an awful lot of people that you've never met."

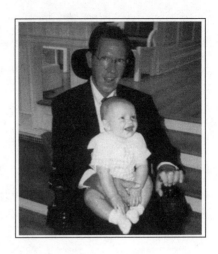

Chapter Eight

THE WORDS AN ALS PATIENT FIRST HEARS about the disease are unbearably harsh. "Terminal," "incurable," a "dread disease" that is always "fatal" in "less than [some small number of] years," a "hopeless," "debilitating" illness that leads to "total paralysis" and effectively "locks the fully conscious patient into a lifeless body" so that one is "living in a glass coffin." And these are the things patients and their families hear from people who are actually trying to help! These are words from doctors, from caregivers, from associations organized to raise awareness and money, and too often from other patients, who have been taught this view of their condition.

Yet there are also patients who know from personal experience that these things, while not exactly lies, are far from the whole truth. Sometimes—often, in fact—they are not the truth at all.

Sportswriter Mitch Albom's best-selling book, *Tuesdays with Morrie*, is a wonderfully touching discovery of life's values under the tutelage of ALS patient and sociology professor Morrie Schwartz, whose openly acknowledged deathbed Albom visits on a succession of Tuesdays. It is an inspiring and uplifting book for people confronting someone else's death, for people whose good health and good fortune have created runaway lives in which values have become a blur. Morrie's wisdom brings life's values back into focus.

For someone newly diagnosed with ALS, however, reading the book is like facing friendly fire—a deadly attack with weapons in the hands of allies who are presumably aiming at something else. Morrie's ALS diagnosis is announced by Albom as a "death sentence"; that sentence is delivered by a doctor who says, "I'm sorry but, yes, you are going to die." Every ALS patient in the world has met that doctor or a classmate of his from the Medical School of Doom and, absent some experience to the contrary, will read this as confirmation of a hopeless prognosis.

Albom erroneously reports five years "from contracting the disease" as the outer limits of a patient's life, never mind that no one knows when the disease is "contracted." On top of that, the doctors "give" Morrie just two years to live. So convinced is Morrie that he goes them one better, announcing to his class just a month after his diagnosis that he has a "fatal illness" and may not survive the semester. "Brutal," "unforgiving," "terminal," says Albom of ALS, a "slow insidious decay" that reduces its victim to a "soul imprisoned in a limp husk, a man frozen inside his own flesh." Try digesting *that* after being diagnosed with the disease.

When I read about Morrie, I was about to enter the fifth spring since my diagnosis. I remember being surprised by the first spring. In the winter months after the diagnosis, I had carefully pruned every bush and vine in the yard so that Joan could show someone how it should be done when I could no longer do it. Then spring came. The shrubbery sprouted new growth, and, since there was really nothing wrong with me, I had to prune it all again. And again. I had also pulled up all the flowers that required special attention I would no longer be able to give them—roses that would have to be trimmed and fertilized and sprayed, chrysanthemums that would have to be cut back regularly until the Fourth of July. But spring came, and I could work the garden as well as ever. When I planted already-blooming annuals for an "instant garden," I felt reasonably confident that I would be around at the end of the season and be able to clean them up.

My mother had given me a bundle of switches for Christmas. She thought it was a hoot. After she finished laughing, she said, "Put them in a jar of water; they'll sprout roots. Plant them when it gets warm out, and they'll bloom in November." At the time, I had not allowed myself to think as far ahead as the next November, but I put the dead sticks in a jar. Through the winter months, the jar filled with long, hairy, green roots. In April, I planted the sticks in a place where I would be able to see them bloom from inside the house, since I might be unable to go outside by November.

About the time my mother gave me those dead sticks that she promised would eventually dazzle me with flowers, I got a telephone call at the office from someone I didn't know. Her name was Betty White, and she had just heard about my diagnosis from a mutual friend. "I just wanted you to know that my father had ALS," she said. *Had.* I caught the verb tense, but she plowed ahead. "He had it for twelve years," she said. Better, but still past tense. "He would have had it longer, but he died of a heart attack." I'm afraid I laughed out loud, but it must have been all right. When she continued, I felt certain I heard a chuckle. "You don't have to talk about it now," she said, "but I just wanted to tell you two things. One: Don't panic. And two: Watch your cholesterol!" After the briefest of good-byes, she was gone.

A total stranger had reached out and touched me with a wonderfully comforting hug—either that or angels had learned to use telephones.

Joan's mother was another comforter. "Don't you worry," she said, patting me on the head through the long telephone line from Minneapolis. "Everything is going to be all right." Mothers say that. Joan's mother believed it.

I decided that, at the very least, everything *else* was going to be all right, starting with cholesterol. I went to see Bill Bullock, our family physician. I reminded him that, although I had been handed off to neurologists for the ALS, he was still in charge of everything else. We agreed that we would do everything we could to keep the rest of me as healthy as possible. He gave me a thorough exam and sent me the results with a wonderful letter. "I know this sounds odd," he wrote, "but you're in perfect health."

(Four years later, he was still insisting there was nothing wrong with me except for ALS, which was not his area of responsibility.)

The dead sticks from my mother took root in the backyard. In fact, they very nearly took flight, growing to a height of eight feet before summer was out. In November, blossoms that looked like camellia buds opened into huge, roselike flowers that were easily visible from the house. But I was still going outside, and I still had to prune them myself. I felt so good about it that I broke off some sticks and put them in a jar of water for the next year. And I planted bulbs that would bloom in the spring, the second spring since my diagnosis. Having been surprised by one spring, I was now actually preparing for one yet to come.

In the second spring, while I was cutting the new daffodils—and pruning the shrubbery again—I began planning a new garden at the lake. This time, I took the long view: perennials. I began to think of springs to come. Plural.

By the third spring, when the perennial garden was ready for planting, I needed some help carrying flats of flowers and digging holes to put them in. But I could still shop. I bought hundreds of plants—hundreds more than I could possibly plant by myself. I had read laments on the Internet from ALS patients who said the disease had robbed them of the joy of gardening, and I was determined that I would at least have the joy of a complete garden in place. During the course of that spring, however, I discovered an ancient and enlightening truth about gardening: "The *joy of gardening* is nothing as compared to the *joy of giving orders in the garden*." Neal and Mary, my brother and sister-in-law whose summer house is across the cove from ours, came to the rescue. Neal declared himself the director of home improvements and repairs; Mary took over the garden. With help from Andy and then Neil and Jamie and Rusty and anyone who happened by, Mary planted, weeded, pruned, and clipped. Soon, we had an incredibly beautiful perennial garden.

By the fourth spring, the flowers had spread out and bloomed like a mature garden. Even brother Bubba—"Dr. Bubba" to strangers, the oldest and strongest and smartest and most ornery of the Martin boys, whose love for flowers and tolerance for emotion made those traits acceptably manly around our house— was impressed. And for the first time in our married life, Joan took an interest in the garden. She began bringing in armloads of flowers and arranging them in vases for nearly every room in the house. Until then, flowers for the house had been my job alone, and I now enjoyed her interest in the garden as much as I enjoyed the flowers themselves.

I could hardly wait for the next spring, the fifth since my diagnosis. Just as I had once been encouraged by a succession of sunrises to begin considering the possibilities of days to come, I now began considering the possibilities of future springs. Those springs-to-come gave me confidence and expectation, but it was the spring at hand that filled me—that filled *us*—with the joy of life.

That's where I was, anticipating yet another beautiful spring, when I read *Tuesdays with Morrie* and confronted the philosophical old man with ALS who believed he was dying and set about doing just that. That's where I was when I learned that Jack Kevorkian was helping ALS patients commit suicide, the premise being that the public would understand because the life of these patients was so obviously hopeless, so bleak, so terrifying that they should not have to live another day, let alone another spring. And that's where I was when the question of life support became a relevant and timely issue in my life.

Without planning to arrive at that day, I had. Life support, life expectancy, quality of life, will to live—all those phrases that were so easy to handle in the abstract suddenly became a concrete wall. And written on the wall was not a prophesy or an instruction, but a question directed at me: "Will you live like this?"

Where was the decision-tree for such a question? What was the logical sequence for reaching a conclusion? Should my will to live be subject to conditions? And given my circumstances, what would reasonable conditions be? The touchstones of life support and life expectancy and quality of life and will to live turned to sand when I tried to hold on to them.

Funny thing about love, hope, faith, joy, laughter, festivity, sense of purpose, determination, and will to live: they seem so intertwined, so interdependent, and yet any one of them can crash while the others are still strong. Each one requires constant monitoring and tending.

I have had friends with medical and other traumas whose gritty determination and will to live carried them through but left their lives diminished, scarred with a lack of love and laughter. I have had friends—particularly friends with ALS—whose lives were full of love and hope and faith and joy and all the rest but who were unwilling to live "like this."

Given an option, these friends declined treatments that would have cured or compensated for some immediate life-threatening complication but would have left them and their families still living with ALS. This they rejected. Sometimes, they left behind bright and beautiful memories of their love and laughter and determination. It cannot be said that they let ALS ruin their lives, even though it is clear that it took their lives.

And it is clear to me that the will to live with an incurable and irreversible condition begins with a willingness to live "like this."

So what is it like, to live "like this"?

Statistically, there is nothing the least bit remarkable about my case of ALS. Though the disease varies widely from individual to individual, I am precisely the norm. The onset of the illness appeared in my limbs at age fifty-three, followed by two years of negligible physical symptoms but substantial psychological challenge, followed by a difficult year of inexorable "progress" of paralysis from my toes to my tongue, followed by more than a year now of stable but unavoidable reality, in which I am unable to walk or talk, to reach or pull, to type or telephone, to hug or pucker for a kiss.

The list of things I *can* do would be far longer—or at least long enough. And some things, after all, are actually better when done slowly and deliberately, with extended anticipation.

Now that I know what "like this" is like, my days are filled with activity, with love and laughter, with purpose and determination—and with anger and irritability at the same things that made me angry and irritable before I ever thought about ALS, things like bigotry and pretense and Duke losses to Carolina.

One late-summer day in 1998, Nancy and Neil (who could both translate my mumbles) left the office with me for a walk (they walked, I drove my wheelchair) up North Tryon Street (they sweated, I didn't), through the district that all of us at the bank have worked so hard to revive. We looked at construction projects, we stepped (they stepped, I wheeled) into an art gallery, we smiled at people on the sidewalk, and they smiled back. Sometimes, strangers could not resist the impulse to pat my shoulder or, worse, my driving hand, which invited a sidewalk catastrophe when my chair lurched in the direction of the pat.

We stopped at an Irish pub for lunch. I had long since decided that I would take the risk of letting people see me, bib and all, being fed by someone. The alternative was to stay home. I found that if I tried to avoid eye contact or to hide, people would stare. But if I smiled and nodded to them, they would always smile and nod back—or give me a wave or a thumbs-up—and we would then all go about our business in a perfectly normal way, "like this."

On the way back to the office, satisfied by the construction excitement, by the art in the gallery, by the smiles and pats on the sidewalk, and by the cider at the pub, I said to Neil and Nancy, "If anybody ever asks you how long I can live 'like this,' the answer is, 'A long time.'"

Life expectancy had shifted for me. Joan's father turned ninety after I began to use a wheelchair, and we reflected on the example of his life. He had been born in a two-room Minnesota log cabin, so premature and small that his Swedish mother and

Norwegian father put him in a cigar box snuggled against the fireplace. He lived and prospered, achieving a level of wealth and prominence in one generation, he genially reminded me, that had taken my family ten generations. I did not tell him that we were still playing catch-up.

What I wanted to tell him, had he not requested no speeches at his birthday party, was that he had set a new standard for life expectancy, and that it had nothing to do with living ninety years. It had to do with the civic and religious projects and institutions he had initiated and nurtured. It had to do with trust and loyalty and integrity. And it had to do with his love for his family and friends and community.

It is of no consequence to me or to anyone else that the population of one country has longer life expectancy than the population of another. What matters is the life expectancy I have for today. John Werness, Joan's father, expected every day to present opportunities for service and for satisfaction. And so they did. On any given day, it isn't the *length* of our life expectancy but its *strength* that will make a difference.

Then came the issue of the feeding tube. After a sinus infection put me in the hospital, the director of our new ALS center in Charlotte, Dr. Jeffrey Rosenfeld, told me that we should not risk another bout with anything that might prevent me from eating and cause me to lose weight. A feeding tube inserted through the wall of my abdomen (more of a cushion than a wall by then) would do the trick. "Best to get it as soon as you're strong again," he said, "rather than waiting until you need it." I agreed, but I wanted the security blanket of the Houston team I had known for more than four years.

The issue of life support seemed to be reserved for ventilators, which assisted with breathing. But it seemed to me that when that time came, it would not be different from questions I was already answering. At one time, the wheelchair had amounted to life support. I could decline it as artificial or mechanical or confining, or I could accept it as the only way to keep on living "like this." Truth is, "like this" actually improved with the chair; I was liberated from the paralysis of my legs.

The feeding tube seemed to me to be in the same category. I would need it if I continued to be willing to live "like this." Nobody on my Houston team had yet asked about life support or a mechanical ventilator. But Dr. Rosenfeld was clear; if I wanted to be in the best condition possible whenever that question came up, I would need the feeding tube now. In truth, Jeffrey Rosenfeld ran the Charlotte clinic according to several basic premises. The clinic could show people how to live "like this." With the sponsorship of the Muscular Dystrophy Association—the people responsible for Jerry Lewis's annual telethon—it could do that at no cost to patients for regular clinic visits. Whatever "like this" turned out to be, the clinic could help people maintain the best quality of life possible. Life, not disease or disability or death, was the expectation that powered the clinic.

The night before we left for Houston, Joan and I attended the wedding of Chuck and Bonnie Cooley's son. Because I would need help, Chuck had made it clear that I was the only wedding guest invited to bring both a spouse and a significant other. So we arrived at the uptown Mint Museum of Craft + Design: Joan and Joe and Rusty. After the ceremony, we gathered on the roof garden of the museum, surrounded by the glittering new towers of Bank of America, slices of the tree-shaded, Victorian Fourth Ward visible between the buildings. The three of us sat at a table with Gerald and Nancy Dry and Hugh and Jane McColl.

"No doubt about it," said Hugh as we looked at the view, "this is our town. And we've done a pretty good job with it." There was no argument from anyone at that table, even when he added, "But we've still got a lot to do." I heard it as a perfect send-off for my encounter with the surgeon.

I had not planned to eat at the wedding reception, but Rusty proclaimed the crab casserole, the baked salmon, and the tenderloin all moist and tender enough for me to handle. He made this proclamation only after he had eaten all the tenderloin on his plate and on mine, but the crab and salmon he helped me eat were perfect. For a guy about to get a feeding tube, I had a doozie of a last meal.

⚘

Joe's celebrations now are labors of love in which he leans on others for help. They are part of what Joe calls "living like this," the "stable but unavoidable reality" of a man unable to perform so many of the functions the rest of us take for granted. Here is Joe, who cannot walk or talk, reach or pull, type or telephone, hug or kiss, contemplating yet another superhuman effort to permit the continuance of his humanity. His medical team wants to put him on a feeding tube, which for Joe comes perilously close to "life support."

For the majority of us, life support consists of the carbon dioxide–oxygen cycle of plants, the water cycle, the food chain, civilization, culture, family, friends, and job. Joe has learned to reinforce those customary supports, adding a strut here, a buttress there, to keep his physical life from collapsing. He persists because life, God's gift to Joe, is a thing so worthy of support. Joe will go on being the good steward, willing himself to live.

In a 1995 letter to son Joe B., Joe wrote, "The truly life-threatening aspect of this disease is not that it can end my life, even though it can, but rather that it might ruin it in the meantime. So the challenge to me is not to avoid eventual death, but to avoid letting its prospect ruin my life or the lives of people around me, now or then."

In fact, it was quite early in his contention with ALS that Joe put himself on life support—the life support of faith. "For people of faith," he told Joe B., "God offers victory over death. . . . I believe victory over death is offered to us now, in the midst of life. It is a victory over fear, a victory over despair, a victory over grief, a victory over those forces that can ruin our lives."

The card beside his bed "shamelessly combines the Psalms and Cal Ripken," declaring, "This is the day the Lord has made: Get up, go to the ballpark, and do your very best." For Joe, no day can be unworthy of living. "And when, some morning, I do not wake up, that will still be the day the Lord has made," he wrote. "With that assurance, I go to sleep without fear. I look forward to the morning with confidence. And I spend my days with all the 'love, hope, faith, joy, laughter, festivity, sense of purpose, determination, and will to live' that my family and friends and I can find."

Sometime before the trip to Houston for the feeding tube, Joan found herself contemplating her husband's stubborn will to live. "What any person needs," she decided then, "is someone who just loves you. I feel like if you have someone that just loves you to pieces . . . Well, it would be really easy to lose your will to live if you didn't have someone like that.

"Joy, love, hope, all of them, I think those add up to the will to live. They make you want to go forward. I often think of how comparatively lucky we are with ALS, because Joe doesn't hurt. He is not in pain. And that, I think—being in real pain—could make you lose your will to live."

Recalling the man with ALS whose euthanasia was aided by Jack Kevorkian and televised by CBS, Joan reflected, "That man was simply afraid that he was going to choke to death, the same way Joe used to be afraid. That poor guy Kevorkian did in! He didn't have anybody telling him, 'It is just normal to be depressed. Let's do something about it. You can take some medicine; we've got that.'" Sometimes, Joan concluded, friends and family must step in to provide the life support of love, determination, and sense of purpose, else our will to live may not endure. And sometimes, life support comes in small packages.

"I think Joe's sadness in the very beginning was knowing we were going to have this grandchild; he wanted to be a grandpa. And now he is. And it is so wonderful. I just talked to Joseph on the phone the other day. He calls me Noni. I just love it; I could melt. He knows he is talking to me. I said, 'Will you come see us at our house?' And he said, 'Yessss.' He always says 'Yessss.' And I said, 'And see PopPop?' And he said, 'PopPop! PopPop! PopPop!' He loves Joe. 'And have a ride on the elevator?' 'Yessss.' Me, I'm fine, but PopPop and the elevator, he just adores.

"For Joe, a will to live is to be able to play with his grandchildren. At Christmas, he and baby Benjamin did this eye-blinking thing all over the place. And Joseph would touch him and run and go back and forth. They would just laugh. Being PopPop is so wonderful. Wouldn't you want to live for that? All those things add up to the will to live. If you have that, you want to live.

"But I think it is awfully nice to have someone who loves you. Really loves you."

Chapter Nine

A T THE METHODIST HOSPITAL in Houston, Joan and I—and Neil—checked into the Neurosensory Intensive Care Unit and were greeted by several of our old teammates from the clinic staff. Given the possibility of respiratory complications, however remote, I was glad to see Dr. Cartrell Cross, the pulmonologist whose knowledge and demeanor had given me confidence through four years of clinic visits.

Stan Appel, by now my trusted friend, had a single question, which he prefaced but never quite asked. "We do not expect to have any problem," he said, "but there is always the possibility that complications with breathing will necessitate an immediate decision about mechanical assistance. We will follow your wishes, but you will have to tell us before we start, since you will be asleep if the question arises."

"My feeling," I said without any memorable emotion, "is that I would choose to have any procedure or treatment that enables us to maintain my life at or near its current quality." I listened very carefully to be sure Neil repeated exactly what I said. He got it right.

Dr. Appel did not take sides. He indicated neither approval nor disapproval. "Very well," he said to the ICU nurse, "we will be fully prepared to do whatever is necessary." Then he said to me, "Don't worry, you're going to be fine."

Joan asked over and over if Neil could stay with me, as a comfort to her and to me, since he alone could interpret my facial signals. Over and over, she was told that hospital policy would not permit it and that, in any event, I would not be sending any signals. But when Joan left to go to the waiting room, she posted Neil in the doorway, where he could see everything.

As the anesthesia was started, someone asked, "Code?"

The ICU nurse answered, "Full code." She looked down at me and explained, "Vent if necessary."

I saw Neil's face in the doorway. I saw Dr. Cross grin and wave "nighty-night."

Someone I did not see said again, "Full code."

Anyone who has had a feeding tube put in will think the drama of my account is preposterous. We are talking about something that takes maybe fifteen minutes and is often done as an outpatient procedure. ALS patients are sometimes kept in the hospital overnight just to be sure there are no respiratory complications, but that's all there is to it.

My situation was a little unusual because of my vulnerability to laryngeal spasms—that is, even though I was fully sedated, my throat would likely clamp down on the tube as it was pushed in, thereby shutting off the flow of oxygen. (Those spasms may be related to ALS, but I suspect genetics. The same thing happened to brother Jim when he last tried to swallow a raw oyster, a terrifying feat that he has not even attempted for at least forty years.)

Inserting the tube was a snap. I felt nothing and was aware of nothing, although Neil reported that the doctor talked to me the whole time, swiftly shuttling tubes and tracer lights and a camera and guide-cords in and out of my stomach through my gullet and through the small incision in my belly. Neil watched the television monitor, where he could see the camera sliding down my esophagus and into my stomach. "Pinkish," he said later, pretty much like in his anatomy book.

I paid absolutely no attention to the procedure and have no memory of it. At the end, I felt so good and was so happy to see everybody again, all standing precisely where I had left them and all smiling, that I looked around the room and said thank you to each of them. Neil translated over and over.

The next morning, I asked if I could get up and sit in my chair. I was ready to leave. No sooner was I up than the color drained from my face, the energy drained from my body, and I felt so lightheaded that I could not speak—could only look at Joan and hope she saw that something was wrong. It was obvious. She and the nurse managed to get me back into bed without an ounce of effort or help from me. My blood pressure had dropped dramatically, and the oxygen level in my blood was dangerously low. My temperature went up.

Try as I might, I cannot now make this sound as bad as it seemed at the time. The facts just don't support my negative reaction. It is possible that the downward spiral of that day was more psychological than physical, but there is no doubt that it was downward. By nightfall, my stomach hurt, the incision hurt, the tube hurt, my head hurt, even my leg hurt where some anesthetic had been injected during the procedure. I was on oxygen, and I was on intravenous feeding for nutrition, liquids, and antibiotics. No one would give me anything to drink or eat, even though I was starving and had negotiated with Stan Appel a general dispensation for eating. "Oh, no," said four different people eight different times, "Dr. Appel never lets his patients take anything by mouth." My throat and mouth were so dry that I could not even try to talk without coughing, so it was not much of a debate. Every single person who came in wanted to explain why I should not eat: there was a possibility of choking, a risk of aspiration, danger of pneumonia. I failed to see how any of that could be worse than what I was already experiencing.

The whole bottom part of my rib cage hurt, and everything hurt worse when I exhaled. Shallow breathing reduced the pain but probably made my general condition worse. I refused even to attempt the breathing exercises that were ordered. I had perfectly good reasons: (a) It hurt, and (b) refusing proved that I was still in control of something. They could withhold food, but they could not make me breathe.

Still, they had all the aces. They told us they could not be certain when I might leave the hospital, but it would not be as early as Thursday, when we had planned to fly home. We should cancel our airline reservations, they said. That was the worst downer yet. I felt very far from home.

Joan suffered through the day with me, alternating between compassion at my discomfort and dismay at my whining. She stifled whatever advice she may have wanted to give and just did whatever I asked. It had to be hard on her. When no one was looking, and without my asking, she wet a cloth and let me chew on it. This didn't provide enough water to force a swallow, but enough to get rid of the dryness in my mouth.

Neil took over for night duty. I did not sleep much, and I did not let him sleep much. I kept asking him to turn me over, then kept letting him know how much it hurt me when he did. Neil's strength enabled him to be steady and gentle—no sudden hefting or shoving. He was better at handling me than any health-care professional we had run into. But I was not about to tell him so on that night. Worse for him, every time he turned me, he needed to change the diapers I had to wear and the sheets I kept wetting. If anybody had a right to whine, it was Neil. But he said nothing. He just did what needed to be done and then waited for the next call.

"Like this" had taken a bad turn. I thought of Billy Anderson, the NFL veteran whose diagnosis at the same time as mine had made me think we would fight this thing side by side. Billy fought, but the truth is that Billy never liked any part of living "like this." He didn't like being in a wheelchair or having to ride a scooter. He didn't like having to be fed. He didn't like having to be turned over at night.

He was surrounded by love from his family and friends, and

he returned that love in full. But when the time came—by way of a bout with pneumonia—to choose between life on a ventilator and a peaceful death, Billy let go. Letting go is not the same thing as giving up. Somehow, the willingness to live must be balanced against a willingness to die. Billy Anderson wanted to live, but he let go at a time that seemed right to him.

I had not understood Billy's choice at the time. But that dark night in the hospital, affected by what turned out to be low-grade pneumonia, I understood.

In *Tuesdays with Morrie*, Mitch Albom reports an easy, do-it-yourself test a doctor told Morrie to use to judge the pace of his approaching death; he could do so, the doctor said, just by breathing and timing the length of forced pauses between breaths. It seemed odd to me when I read it, and I deliberately did not try it then. But in the dark hospital room in Houston, when no one was watching, I took the test. The result showed that I was already dead.

The test confirmed my impression that I could begin shutting down my system just by letting go. But the test overreached. Morrie's doctor might think I was dead, but I was demonstrably not dead. There was a serious flaw in somebody's attitude. Why would the doctor want Morrie or me to think we were beyond the possibility of life? What business does a doctor have with my death? That is not what I needed from a doctor.

So whose business is my death? Apparently, mine. And to whom am I accountable for my decision? To God, who gave me life, on terms that were not of my choosing then and not of my choosing now. How could I impose conditions on my willingness to accept that gift? And as for the family and friends who shared life with me, who were doing their best to support me, and who were willing to accept me "like this," how could I tell them it was not enough?

I thought of Joan in her hotel room across the street, resting from a wearying day with me just so she could come back and go through the same thing again, if need be. That love was the love of the marriage vow, "In sickness and in health," a commitment I had also made to her, not knowing it would be my sickness and not hers. How could I tell her that I had not known it would be "like this," that my present life was not what I had intended with that vow?

I also thought of the cartoon Bob Stone had overnighted me when he heard of my diagnosis: a small green frog halfway down the gullet of a tall heron, but with his arms sticking out and his hands locked in a choke hold around the heron's neck. The caption: "Never give up!"

On my very first trip to the Houston clinic, I had faxed that cartoon back to the bank. Hugh McColl took a look at it and concluded, "I think it means that he has a frog in his throat." Hugh, who had already guided his bank into position as the third largest in the country, could not possibly identify with the endangered frog. In his mind, it was all about the marauding heron. But the point was still the same: Never give up.

I had seen Hugh accomplish astounding things just by refusing to fail. In 1988, we acquired a bank that was larger than ours, and we acquired it by using its own money. The whole premise was preposterous, and the process was predictably tortured. Time and again, when the rest of us would have let go, Hugh persisted. He had no better grasp of the deal than anyone else, and no less an understanding of reality. But having arrived at the point where we were, he refused to let go. In my view, he *willed* the deal to happen. And in everybody's view, that deal led us to possibilities that even Hugh had not imagined.

In fact, the company has been built on possibilities—and more than a few *im*possibilities—in the belief that persistent forward movement will necessarily create new opportunities. Give up, and the possibilities vanish. Likewise, a willingness to live "like this" is not enough. Without an active *will* to live in the face of difficulty or depression or despair, without the will to keep moving forward, willingness will not be an option.

Anger is not on the list of love, hope, faith, joy, laughter, and so on, but it is one way out of depression. By morning, I was mad. When nurse Debbi Otie came in, I told her so. Debbi is an energetic and attractive Irish-Cherokee Texan who lives with her husband and daughters and assorted farm animals out in the country near a small town with the Texas-style name of Splendora. Like all great nurses, Debbi is smart, tough, and loving. When I said I was angry, she pulled up a chair and asked me to tell her about it. I unloaded.

I told her that getting the tube had been a big mistake. I told her that I was being turned into an invalid prematurely, that they were doing the very thing they had told me not to do: anticipating a problem I didn't have. I told her that the concern about my choking was absurd, that I had been eating just fine before they messed me up with this tube, that I had been holding my weight and feeling good as recently as last week. I told her that, though they were now afraid of giving me soup or juice, I had been at a wedding dinner just three days earlier eating crab casserole and baked salmon and drinking good wine. And I told her that I felt double-crossed about the whole deal, since I had been assured that I would still be able to eat after getting the tube and was now getting nothing but lectures about not eating. I told her that I was going to eat, that I was going to prove I could eat, even if leaving the hospital was the only way to get the chance.

Joan was translating for me, but Debbi was paying such close attention that she began picking up words on her own. Before I finished complaining, she was able to repeat to me everything I said. "I will discuss all this with the doctor," she said, "and we'll see what we can do." She went out and returned with a glass of water. "I found this," she said. "Want a sip?"

When Neil came in, he reported that he had called Nancy Dry about changing our airline reservations. Nancy told him she would just cancel them and send the corporate G-5 jet to pick us up on Saturday. There was no way to know whose authority Nancy had. In our company, people make decisions that they believe to be right and then live with the consequences.

In any event, it sounded to me like the bugles of the cavalry in the distance, riding to the rescue. All the philosophy about letting go or not, about quality of life and willingness to live "like this," all of that paled in the light of reality. I knew Nancy, and I knew she would be seriously irritated if I did not get on that plane on Saturday. I began to focus on getting better.

I suppose I would have gotten better anyway. I had the best medical care in the world, and my doctors would have been seriously embarrassed to lose a patient to a tube insertion. In any event, I did get better. I went on living "like this."

Actually, more like this: Being fed (through my two-week-old tube, along with Oreo cookies and a Hershey bar by mouth) beside the trout stream in the Poconos, making up games with Joseph and Benjamin, being with friends at their important family events, going to church and to the office, laughing with our children and applauding their accomplishments, sitting in the garden at the lake, holding Joan's hand.

How many times will I have to learn the lesson? *We do not know what is possible.* Give up, and the possibilities will vanish.

We had decided that Joan would go to Norway without me for the August wedding of her cousin Siri Kavli's son. But by early summer, I had regained my strength, and I felt I could go, too. The tube would actually make travel easier by removing the hassle of finding food I could swallow, while still letting me taste whatever I wanted to. My rule for Norway: Nutrition and medicines swiftly down the tube, rømmegrøt porridge and all desserts slowly down the gullet.

Using my Eyegaze computer, I chatted with Norwegian hotel managers via the Internet, made plans and reservations, and discovered that Norway is remarkably accessible. Hotels, taxivans, trains, boats, and more than enough mountain trails are fitted for wheelchairs. But there was one drawback we would discover: cobblestone streets, which must surely be the original definition of "hell on wheels."

We also discovered that Norwegians know how to combine tradition and fun. Seeing our own Neil dressed for the wedding in their national costume, from the long white coat and silver-scabbarded hunting knife to the knickers and silver-buckled shoes, waltzing (waltzing!) in the first dance of the evening, was worth the cost and effort of the whole trip—well, that and hearing Norwegians and Americans singing along with the groom as he led his own band through what would pass that night as our national anthem, "American Pie."

The following week, we were at Opheim on the Nordfjord, the farm that has been home to Joan's mother's family for five hundred years and is surely one of the most beautiful spots on the face of the earth. We looked at the fjord eight hundred feet below us and at mountains eight thousand feet high on the other side, framing the crystal-blue Briksdal glacier. We were surrounded by the sound of waterfalls, the tinkling bells of mountain sheep, and the chatter of a family that was incredibly loving to relatives from so far away. I was struck by how good I felt, and I resolved that if I ever found myself fighting pneumonia and depression again, I would think of Opheim.

But life doesn't have to be like that. "Like this" is good enough: Sitting by the fire at home again with Joan, keeping up with everybody by way of the computer, anticipating a new crop of daffodils, and getting ready for another Duke run to the NCAA tournament. Not a bad place to start yet another year.

James Keller, the San Antonio baseball coach and ALS patient we met on our first visit to the Houston clinic, told us that one reason he liked baseball was that there is no clock.

In baseball, he said, you keep playing—and you keep playing to win—until the final out.

It does not matter that the bases are loaded against you in the bottom of the ninth inning, with the score tied, and no outs. When the next batter steps up, third baseman Cal Ripken has a single thought in his head: *The play is at home.*

One out, then two more. Then you are back at bat, the game goes on, and the possibilities are wide open.

✦

Dawn of the year 2000 yawned under a heavy quilt of fog, as though all the smoke from all the fireworks of Europe had billowed across the Atlantic in advance of the sun and piled against the head-board of the Blue Ridge Mountains. The Carolina Piedmont, where Charlotte lies, was nearly invisible and mostly asleep.

Rubbing the millennium celebration from my eyes, clutching my coffee mug, I stumbled to my computer, whose name is Lillian. As soon as her screen glowed to life, I knew Lillian had survived the threatened Y2K techno-holocaust. The big news on the Internet was that there was no big news; we had survived into the next thousand years.

Checking my America Online buddy list, I saw no sign of Joe Martin. But that was not unusual. Joe does much of his best computer communing by night and often doesn't log on again until late in the morning. Since my own computer and coffee maker had made it into 2000, I was confident that Joe's life support—Eyegaze and Internet, power chair and feeding tube, family and personal staff—had achieved twenty-first-century status as well. Before the fog could lift, I suspected, Joe would be at his work station and all would be right with the world.

Two hours later, my optimism was justified by the unmistakable name on the buddy list, the New Age fingerprint of Joe Martin. My mind's eye located him in his customary dark slacks and white shirt, slightly slumped but supporting himself in the cushioned black power chair. Joe's jaws would be clamped around a maroon washcloth, carefully folded and placed there by one of his kind and caring assistants to absorb the drool. He would be concentrating on the screen before him, letter by letter, eyes darting to a secondary screen where the words he assembled would lay themselves out in stark white on black, spelling the thoughts Joe wanted to share on this first day of the year/century/millennium.

But for the bifocals, the washcloth, and the graying hair, his boyish face had barely changed from that of the head cheerleader and student-body vice president who grinned out of the 1958 Dreher High School yearbook from Columbia, South Carolina. A friend of mine, Teddy Kohn, was on the cheerleading squad with Joe, and he brought that yearbook over to give me a look. Nearly a half-century later, after jobs at prestigious colleges and after helping to form America's largest bank, Joe is still leading life's cheering section. Joe is still energizing the student body. Joe is still Joe.

Looking at him today, you can't help but see the rat that is ALS gnawing away at his nerve cells, slinking through his limbs and lungs, but you know for certain the disease is not Joe. There's a man there, a whole man, and you can bet your life that rat never will kill whatever it is that makes Joe. In truth, it's rarely the rats that get any of us—rarely the cancers, the car wrecks, or the heart attacks. More often, it is the killer fleas that ride in on those rats, the carriers of the plague of hopelessness.

Despair is the Black Death, and Joe's defiance of it helps the rest of us know that we can defy it, too. If we cherish love, if we embrace hope, if we celebrate life, then love, hope, and life never will give up on us.

Joe greets every day as though it is the dawn of a new millennium. He logs on to his computer, and only heaven knows who or what he'll find there. He rounds a corner in his motorized chair, and God knows who'll be coming toward him. From the diagnosis of imminent death delivered in the autumn of 1994, Joe continues to recover, continues to heal.

Joe's rule for living, for recovering and healing, is poetic in its simplicity. "This is the day the Lord has made: Get up. Go to the ballpark, and do your very best." Amen.

Some of us are more prosaic. We need things spelled out. We require detailed instructions. I believe those instructions are contained in Joe's mantra, which can be reconstructed into a "ten commandments" of living, healing, and recovering, applicable to all of us.

1

LOVE life and the people important to your life,
without condition, without expectation.

2

HOPE in each moment of every day, because
more things are possible than you can imagine.

3

Have FAITH that God will let you know
about the next life when this one is done.

4

Build JOY out of the materials you find within
the day, with the help of those who
are here to be on your team.

5

Let LAUGHTER embarrass fear and stupidity,
let it heal the hurt in others.

6

Insist upon FESTIVITY, and never
miss a good cause for celebration.

7

Keep your SENSE OF PURPOSE intact,
in sight, and in focus.

8

Let your DETERMINATION be contagious,
expanding geometrically as you add to it the
Determination of others.

9

Make WILL TO LIVE your will to love,
creating a regenerating cycle of power.

10

Until this life truly ends, understand
that on any given day—on this day—
its POSSIBILITIES ARE ENDLESS.

Information on How to Get Help

ALS Association
27001 Agoura Road.
Suite 150
Calabasas Hills, California 91301-5104
(800) 782-4747
http://www.alsa.org

Muscular Dystrophy Association - USA
National Headquarters
3300 E. Sunrise Drive
Tucson, Arizona 85718
(800) 572-1717
http://www.mdausa.org